Byzantine Military Rhetoric in the Ninth Century

Byzantine Military Rhetoric in the Ninth Century is the first English translation of the ninth-century *Anonymi Byzantini Rhetorica Militaris*. This influential text offers a valuable insight into the warrior ethic of the period, the role of religion in the justification of war, and the view of other military cultures by the Byzantine elite. It also played a crucial role in the compilation of the tenth-century Taktika and Constantine VII's harangues during a period of intense military activity for the Byzantine Empire on its eastern borders. Including a detailed commentary and critical introduction to the author and the structure of the text, this book will appeal to all those interested in Byzantine political ideology and military history.

Georgios Theotokis is a lecturer of European history at Ibn Haldun University, Turkey. His publications include *Norman Campaigns in the Balkans, 1081–1108 AD* (2014) and *Byzantine Military Tactics in Syria and Mesopotamia in the Tenth Century* (2018).

Dimitrios Sidiropoulos is currently PhD Student in Byzantine History (Aristotle University of Thessaloniki).

Byzantine Military Rhetoric in the Ninth Century

A Translation of the *Anonymi Byzantini Rhetorica Militaris*

Georgios Theotokis and Dimitrios Sidiropoulos

Routledge
Taylor & Francis Group

LONDON AND NEW YORK

First published 2021
by Routledge
2 Park Square, Milton Park, Abingdon, Oxon OX14 4RN

and by Routledge
52 Vanderbilt Avenue, New York, NY 10017

Routledge is an imprint of the Taylor & Francis Group, an informa business

© 2021 Georgios Theotokis and Dimitrios Sidiropoulos

The right of Georgios Theotokis and Dimitrios Sidiropoulos to be identified as authors of this work has been asserted by them in accordance with sections 77 and 78 of the Copyright, Designs and Patents Act 1988.

British Library Cataloguing-in-Publication Data
A catalogue record for this book is available from the British Library

Library of Congress Cataloging-in-Publication Data
Names: Syrianus, Magister, author. | Theotokis, Georgios, editor. | Sidiropoulos, Dimitrios, 1952– editor.
Title: Byzantine military rhetoric in the Ninth Century : a translation of the Anonymi Byzantini Rhetorica Militaris / Georgios Theotokis, and Dimitrios Sidiropoulos.
Other titles: Rhetorica Militaris. English | Translation of the Anonymi Byzantini Rhetorica Militaris
Subjects: LCSH: Military art and science—Byzantine Empire—Early works to 1800. | Rhetoric—Early works to 1800. | Byzantine Empire—History, Military—527-1081. | War—Early works to 1800.
Classification: LCC DF543 .S97 2021 (print) | LCC DF543 (ebook) | DDC 355.009495/09021—dc23
LC record available at https://lccn.loc.gov/2020053815
LC ebook record available at https://lccn.loc.gov/2020053816

ISBN: 978-0-367-90208-7 (hbk)
ISBN: 978-1-032-00604-8 (pbk)
ISBN: 978-1-003-02311-1 (ebk)

Typeset in Times New Roman
by Apex CoVantage, LLC

Contents

List of figures   vii

Introduction   1
Part A: the author and the work 1
  Syrianos magistros and the compendium of
    Anonymus Byzantinus 1
  Assigning a name to Anonymus Byzantinus 3
  Assigning a date to the compendium of Syrianos 6
  Dating the compendium *and the geo-political*
    background of the period 11
  A note on the sources 21
  The manuscript tradition 25
Part B: the contents of the work 28
  The history of exhortation and exhortative speeches 28
  The "practicalities" of exhortation speeches: where,
    when, how 35
  The skills of a commander as a public speaker 37
  Rhetorical topoi in building morale 39

Note on the translation   55

Hortatory public speeches: drawing their arguments
from various sources   57
For the zeal for the faith 61
For the fatherland 62
For the love for our compatriots 62
For the punishment of evildoers 63

Other made-up arguments 67
From religion 70
From the mode of life 70
From the slander of the enemy army 70
From [the right] time 70
From the place 70
From the cause 70
From the past, in this way 71
From the present, such as 71
From the future, such as 71
From the fabrications, such as 71
The achievements of the audience 72
The achievements of the ancestors of the audience 73
The achievements of others 73
More examples about the useful 77
  The preparation of weapons 77
The training in war tactics 78
Bravery 79
The endurance of pain 79
The obedience to the commanders 79
The study of the glorious 80
The study of the possible 80
The study of the outcome of the battle 81
Example of a consolatory speech, in the absence of
  the transposition of the cause [when the reproach
  takes place, then the transposition of the cause is
  missing] 87

Bibliography   88
A Primary sources 88
B Secondary sources 88
Index - introduction   93
Index - translation   95
Index - Greek terms   96

Figures

1.1   Map of the Mediterranean   17
1.2   Gaius (Caligula). Struck AD 40–41.   33
1.3   Galba. Struck circa December AD 68.   34

Introduction

Part A: the author and the work

Syrianos magistros and the compendium of Anonymus Byzantinus

Syrianos magistros has been attributed as the author of a comprehensive treatise that was published as three separate works broadly covering all aspects of warfare [τακτικά, δημηγορίαι, ναυμαχικά]:[1] the *On Strategy* (*De re strategica*),[2] which began with some general observations about the body politic before quickly turning to the topic that really interested the author and "which is really the most important branch of the entire science of government," strategy; the *Rhetorica militaris*, which is a comprehensive general's guidebook on how to compose and deliver rhetorical speeches for the exhortation of the troops before and up to the point of battle and, finally, the *Naumachiae*,[3] which covers various topics related to strategy and tactics at

1 In the *On Strategy*, the author explains that: "There are two kinds of war, at sea and on land. The tactics appropriate to each must be examined separately. . . . To avoid confusion, then, we shall discuss each form of warfare by itself, taking land warfare first" [*On Strategy*, ch. 14]. Bearing in mind that naval warfare and the fleet are not dealt with in the *On Strategy*, we can only assume that the section promised by the author is the *Naumachiae*. On top of that, at the beginning of the *Rhetorica Militaris*, the author claims he wishes to examine the "oral" or "verbal" part, as opposed to the "practical" part, of the political science he has already examined in detail: *Rhetorica Militaris*, I. 1.

2 G. T. Dennis, *Three Byzantine Military Treatises*, CFHB: 25 [Washington, DC: Dumbarton Oaks, 1985/2008 (repr.)], 10–135.

3 A. Dain, *Naumachica* (Paris: Les Belles Lettres, 1943), 43–55; (English translation), J. H. Pryor and E. M. Jeffreys, *The Age of the ΔΡΟΜΩΝ: The Byzantine Navy ca. 500–1204* (Leiden: Brill, 2006), 455–81; (Greek translation), I. Ch. Demetroukas, Ναυμαχικά Λέοντος Στ΄, Μαυρικίου, Συριανού Μαγίστρου, Βασιλείου Πατρικίου, Νικηφόρου Ουρανού [*Naumachica of Leo VI, Maurice, Syrianos Magister, Basil Patrikios, Nikephoros Ouranos*] (Athens: Kanake, 2005), 111–43; (Italian translation), F. Corazzini, *Scritto sulla Tattica Navale di Anonimo Greco* (Livorno: Vannini, 1883).

sea. Historians have proposed that the *compendium* may also have included a section on siege warfare no longer extant.[4] The assertion of the common authorship of the *On Strategy* and the *Rhetorica Militaris* goes as far back as the seventeenth century, when the German philologist, geographer and historian from Hamburg, Lukas Holste (1596–2 February 1661), first suggested it in a manuscript notation, adding that the first work (i.e. *On Strategy*) represented the πρακτικόν μέρος (i.e. the "practical" part) and the second (i.e. *Rhetorica Militaris*) accounted for the λογικόν μέρος (i.e. the "logical" or "verbal" part) of the *De Orationibus Militaribus Tractatus*.[5] Yet it was because of the editorial and translation work of two great scholars of the nineteenth century, Hermann Köchly and Wilhelm Rüstow – the first editors of both manuals – that Holste's idea took hold.[6] Furthermore, it was Köchly and Rüstow who coined the term *Anonymus Byzantinus*. Finally, the "common paternity" of all three works of the *compendium* of the so-called *Anonymus Byzantinus* was supported a quarter of a century later by Karl Konrad Müller, who, in 1882, also attributed the *Naumachiae* to the same author as the aforementioned two, in his edition of the Greek text under the title *De proelio navali*.[7]

Nevertheless, it would take another century for the three texts to be treated as one. That was because of a misunderstanding by one of the most influential codicologists of the twentieth century, Alphonse Dain.[8] In 1943, Dain strongly supported the textual independence of the *On Strategy* from the other two works, thus influencing leading scholars of the next generation, like George Dennis, to publish an English translation of the latter treatise, in 1985, as an independent piece of Byzantine military literature of the sixth

---

4   Philip Rance, "The Reception of Aineias' Poliorketika in Byzantine Military Literature," in: Maria Pretzler and Nick Barley (eds.), *Brill's Companion to Aineias Tacticus* (Leiden: Brill, 2017), 290–374 [here: 318, n. 82]; P. Rance, "Tactics and Tactica in the Sixth Century: Tradition and Originality" (Unpublished PhD thesis, University of St. Andrews, St. Andrews, 1994), 59–61.

5   Imma Eramo, "On Syrianus Magister's Military Compendium," *Classica et Christiana* 7 (2012), 97–116 [here: 97–8]; A. Dain, "Luc Holste et la 'Collection Romaine' des Tacticiens grecs," *Revue des Études Anciennes* 71 (1969), 338–53.

6   *On Strategy* was published in H. Köchly and W. Rüstow, *Griechische Kriegsschriftsteller*, vol. II (Leipzig: Engelmann, 1853–1855), Part 2 ['Der Byzantiner Anonymus Kriegswissenschaft']. Köchly's textual connection between the *On Strategy* and the *Rhetorica Militaris* is on pages 14–21, with the full Greek text and German translation on pages 42–209. For the *Rhetorica Militaris* edition: H. Köchly (ed.), *Anonymi Byzantini rhetorica militaris nunc primum edita* (Zürich, 1855–1856).

7   K. K. Müller, *Eine griechische Schrift über Seekrieg* (Würzburg, 1882), with Müller's suggestion of the common authorship on pages 46–9.

8   Dain (1943), especially pages 9–10 and 44.

century. Therefore, it is thanks to the authoritative study by Constantine Zuckerman in 1990 that historians have come to accept beyond reasonable doubt not only the "common paternity" but also Syrianus' authorship of all three of the aforementioned works.[9]

Zuckerman's theory of the "common paternity" of the *compendium* relies primarily on the thematic and stylistic parallels between the three works. For Zuckerman, *Anonymus* applied the same tactical and rhetorical devices when it comes to writing about land and naval warfare, thus dismissing the word-for-word reiteration for the *Naumachiae*, which could have implied that the author of the naval treatise – if different from *Anonymus* – would have drawn and adapted his material from the *On Strategy* or the *Rhetorica Militaris*. Zuckerman identified several points of correspondence between the *Naumachiae* and the *On Strategy*, based on *Anonymus*' concept of land and naval tactics, which is largely shaped by the author's notion of the "phalanx." The naval formation of warships is an adaptation of his description of a land phalanx, while the same principle applies for the author's highlighting of the importance of keeping an orderly formation while on march, for the use of scouts in advance of a phalanx and for equipping the front ranks of a phalanx with the best weaponry available. Furthermore, numerous parallels between the *Naumachiae* and the *Rhetorica Militaris* are drawn from the passages instructing/exhorting the general to battle: both texts deter the general from engaging in battle unless he holds the upper hand over his enemy in both numbers and morale. Finally, while upholding Zuckerman's views on the thematic parallels, Cosentino draws attention to the great number of stylistic affinities between the three texts, mainly concerning the use of the neutral form, common terminologies and grammatical similarities,[10] thus further confirming the "common paternity" of the *compendium*.

Assigning a name to Anonymus Byzantinus

The breakthrough regarding the name of the author of the *compendium* came – once again – by Dain, who was able to demonstrate that he had made out the inscription *ΝΑΥΜΑΧΙΑΙ ΣΥΡΙΑΝΟΥ ΜΑΓΙΣΤΡΟΥ* on folio 332^v of the *Ambrosianus* B-119-sup that includes the *Naumachiae* (fs. 333^r–338^v).[11]

9 C. Zuckerman, "The Military Compendium of Syrianus Magister," *Jahrbuch der Öster-reichischen Byzantinistik* 40 (1990), 209–24.

10 S. Cosentino, "The Syrianos' Strategikon – a 9th-Century Source?" *Bizantinistica: Rivista di studi bizantini e slavi* 2 (2000), 257–8. For more examples, see: Eramo (2012), 105–8.

11 A. Dain, *La "Tactique" de Nicéphore Ouranos* (Paris: Les Belles Lettres, 1937), 67.

Therefore, it is the work of this Syrianos, along with the well-known second-century AD military theoretician Polyaenus, which the emperor Constantine VII Porphyrogennetos advised his son to bring with him on campaign in his mid-tenth-century treatise *On What Should be Observed When the Great and High Emperor Goes on Campaign*.[12] This is another proof of the common authorship of the *Naumachiae* and the *On Strategy*, because it would have been unlikely for Constantine VII to recommend a treatise on naval warfare as paramount reading for his son Romanos on the occasion of the latter's "land" campaign in eastern Asia Minor against the Hamdanid emir of Aleppo. Finally, the name Syrianos also appears (written by a scribe) in the margins of the Viennese codex *Vindobonensis phil. graecus 275* of emperor Leo's *Tactical Constitutions*, along with the names of Arrian, Aelian, Pelops, Onasander, Menas, Polyaenus and Plutarch, in the section of the prologue where the author writes that:

> After devotedly giving our attention to the ancient, as well as to the more recent, strategic and tactical methods, and having read about further details in other accounts, if we came across anything in those sources that seemed useful for the needs of war, we have, as it were, gathered it up and collected it.[13]

Modern historians know surprisingly little about Syrianos magistros, as we find no person with this name in the primary sources between the mid-seventh and tenth centuries.[14] Syrianos' epithet implies that he had been awarded the senior dignity of *magistros*, a title that can be etymologically linked to the earlier office of the *magister officiorum*.[15] The latter was a

---

12 John F. Haldon (ed. and trans.), *Constantine Porphyrogenitus: Three Treatises on Imperial Military Expeditions* (Vienna: Verlag der Österreichischen Akademie der Wissenschaften, 1990), 106.

13 George Dennis (ed. and trans.), *The Taktika of Leo VI* (Washington, DC: Dumbarton Oaks, 2010), prologue 6, 6–7.

14 Cosentino (2000), 275 (n. 157). On the name Syrianos: Imma Eramo, "Romaioi e Arabes a battaglia? Nota al De re strategica di Siriano Magistros," *Invigilata Lucernis* 31 (2009), 96 (n. 4).

15 For the offices of the *Magister Officiorum* and *magistros*: Christopher Kelly, "Magister Officiorum," in: Oliver Nicholson (ed.), *The Oxford Dictionary of Late Antiquity* (Oxford: Oxford University Press, 2018), 943; Christopher Kelly, "Bureaucracy and Government," in: Noel Lenski (ed.), *The Cambridge Companion to the Age of Constantine* (Cambridge: Cambridge University Press, 2006), 183–204 [especially: 188–90]; A. Kazhdan et al. (eds.), *The Oxford Dictionary of Byzantium*, vol. 2 (Oxford: Oxford University Press, 1991), 1267; Manfred Clauss, *Der magister officiorum in der Spätantike (4.-6. Jahrhundert): Das Amt und sein Einfluss auf die kaiserliche Politik* (Munich: Vestigia, 1980);

powerful palatine official, bearing the dignity of *illustris* after 380, that was created by the separate administrations of Constantine I and Licinius shortly after 312 (it is first attested in the sources in 320).[16] He had as his main responsibility the overseeing of the civil and military staff related to the legal, administrative, diplomatic and ceremonial business conducted by the emperor.

By the end of the reign of Leo III (reigned 717–40), however, the greater part of the administrative functions of the office of the *magister officiorum* was transferred to other officials that – up until then – had been subordinates to him. Those included the *Logothete of the Dromos* or Postal Logothete (Greek: λογοθέτης τοῦ δρόμου), the *Quaestor*, the *Domestic of the Schools* (Greek: δομέστικος τῶν σχολῶν), the *Secretary of Petitions* (Greek: ὁ ἐπὶ τῶν δεήσεων) and the *Master of Ceremonies* (Greek: ὁ ἐπὶ της καταστάσεως).[17] Therefore, as Bury very aptly put it, "the μάγιστρος of the eighth century is the *magister officiorum* shorn of most of his old functions,"[18] while the addition τῶν ὀφφικίων (Latin, *officiorum*) was gradually dropped, although Bury also notes the "exceptional" case of Leo VI's (reigned 886–912) powerful father-in-law, Stylianos Zaoutzes, who was recorded in Leo's Novels as μάγιστρος τῶν θείων ὀφφικίων.

Evidence suggest that until the reign of Michael III (reigned 842–67), there seem to have been only two *magistroi*, a title conferred to eminent patricians for life, the senior of whom was termed *prōtomagistros* (πρωτομάγιστρος, literary "first magistros"). The latter was a leading member of the Senate and shared in the decision-making process of the government with the chamberlain and the urban prefect during imperial absences.[19] The second *magistros* participated in the ceremonial duties of the first. Finally, the title was conferred on more holders during the reign of Basil I (reigned 867–86), although certainly fewer than the number 12 implied in the List of Precedence (Klētorologion) of Philotheos, written in 899.[20] By the tenth century, it had effectively transformed into a court dignitary, the highest until the introduction and award of the *prōedros* (Greek: πρόεδρος) by Nikephoros II (reigned 963–69) to Basil Lekapenos.

Arthur Edward Boak, *The Master of the Offices in the Later Roman and Byzantine Empires* (London: Macmillan, 1919/1924); J. B. Bury, *The Imperial Administrative System in the Ninth Century* (London: Oxford University Press, 1911), 29–33.

16 Kelly (2006), 188–9; Kazhdan et al. (1991), 1267; Clauss (1980), 9–14; Boak (1919/1924), 24–8.

17 Boak (1919/1924), 50–1.

18 Bury (1911), 29.

19 Boak (1919/1924), 52–5; Bury (1911), 31.

20 Kazhdan et al. (1991), 1267; Boak (1919/1924), 55–6; Bury (1911), 32.

Assigning a date to the compendium of Syrianos

Historians have at their disposal only two certain historical *termini* that can locate the authorship of the *compendium* in a period that is about three centuries long: the reference to the generalship of Belisarius (AD 530–59) and the use of Syrianos' work in the composition of Leo VI's *Tactical Constitutions* (AD 904–12).

With the "land" treatise *On Strategy* naturally attracting the lion's share of attention, the *compendium* has traditionally been dated to the reign of Justinian (527–65),[21] following Köchly and Rüstow's first edition of 1855 that cited four pieces of internal evidence. First, the author's allusions to the celebration of triumphs in the capital, pointing to Belisarius' famous triumph in the Hippodrome following his reconquest of North Africa in 534; then, the "divide-and-rule" diplomacy of the emperor, which Köchly and Rüstow identified as – clearly – Justinianic in nature; third, the prominence of archery in the text that points more to a sixth-century compilation date rather than later; finally, a reference to the generalship of Belisarios in the present tense.[22] Yet a handful of modern scholars like Barry Baldwin, Doug Lee, Jonathan Shepard, Salvatore Cosentino and Philip Rance have demonstrated beyond reasonable doubt the flimsiness of the arguments that have formed the foundation of the dating for the *compendium* to the sixth century,[23] pointing rather to a much later date sometime in the (later) ninth century.

In 2007, Philip Rance published the latest academic study concerning the debate about the dating of Syrianos' *compendium* in an article that "intended to complement the insights of Baldwin, Lee and Shepard, and Cosentino by identifying five additional dating criteria that are incongruent with a sixth-century date and more consistent with a middle Byzantine context." Therefore, regardless of the fact that historians are still unable

21 Konstantina Karaple, *Κατευόδωσις στρατού: Η οργάνωση και η ψυχολογική προετοιμασία του βυζαντινού στρατού πριν από τον πόλεμο (610–1081)* [*Kateuodosis Stratou: The Organization and Mental Preparation of the Byzantine Army Before War (610–1081)*] (Athens: Myrmidones, 2010), 38 (n. 45); Zuckerman (1990), 216–17; Taxiarches Kolias, *Byzantinische Waffen: Ein Beitrag zur byzantinischen Waffenkunde von den Anfängen bis zur lateinischen Eroberung* (Vienna: Verlag der Österreichischen Akademie der Wissenschaften, 1988), 31; Dennis (1985/2008), 2–3; Dain (1967), 343; J. B. Bury, *History of the Later Roman Empire*, vol. II (London: Macmillan, 1923), 292 (n. 1); Köchly and Rüstow (1853–1855), 37–8.

22 A summary of Köchly and Rüstow's arguments in Philip Rance, "The Date of the Military Compendium of Syrianus Magister (Formerly the Sixth-Century *Anonymus Byzantinus*)," *Byzantinische Zeitschrift* 100 (2007), 708–9.

23 Rance (2007), 708–37; Cosentino (2000), 262–75; A. D. Lee and J. Shepard, "A Double Life: Placing the Peri Presbeon," *ByzantinoSlavica* 52 (1991), 15–39; Barry Baldwin, "On the Date of the Anonymous *Περί στρατηγικῆς*," *Byzantinische Zeitschrift* 81 (1988), 290–3.

to pinpoint the exact year, or even decade, of Syrianos' work, we can say with confidence that a sixth-century date is no longer plausible. And here is why: despite Köchly and Rüstow's confidence that the author referred to Belisarius' famous triumph in the Hippodrome in 534, scholarship on the subject has shown that the celebrations of campaign triumphs with captives in public remained a very common practice until the eleventh century, especially during the period of the "Macedonians."[24] In order to safeguard his position, for example, Emperor Basil I (reigned 867–86) exploited the victory celebrations to the fullest, and, in total, he celebrated three triumphal victories in the capital, the most important of which was his second triumph after the conclusion of his 873 campaign in the East against the heretical Paulicians of Tephrike.[25] Furthermore, Köchly and Rüstow's divide-and-rule foreign policy over Byzantium's neighbours should not be construed as particularly "Justinianic," because it was also very common in the following centuries, especially during the critical tenth century of the Byzantine "Re-conquest" in the East.[26] On top of that, the alleged prominence of archery in the treatise is, surely, not another indication of its Justinianic origin, as archery remained a significant weapon for imperial armies during

---

24 M. McCormick, *Eternal Victory, Triumphal Rulership in Late Antiquity, Byzantium, and the Early Medieval West* (Cambridge: Cambridge University Press, 1986), 144–88.

25 A very interesting case is that of Bardas Phocas' second son, Leo, *strategos* of Cappadocia who, in 956, captured a Hamdanid party led by Sayf ad-Dawla's cousin, Abu'l Asair. According to the *De Ceremoniis* – and in particular a specific section of the second book that was probably compiled between 957 and 959 – we read about the revival of the *calcatio*, a Roman ritual that had not been used in triumphal processions since the crushing of Thomas the Slav's rebellion in 823: McCormick (1986), 161; Constantine Porphyrogenitus, *De Ceremoniis Aulae Byzantinae*, Corpus Scriptorum Historiae Byzantinae, ed. J. J. Reiske, vol. 5–6 (Bonn: Webber, 1829–1830), 607–12.

26 Nike Koutrakou, "Diplomacy and Espionage: Their Role in Byzantine Foreign Relations, 8th–10th Centuries," *Graeco-Arabica* 6 (1995), 125–44; J. Shepard, "Information, Disinformation and Delay in Byzantine Diplomacy," *Byzantinische Forschungen* 10 (1985), 233–93. See also the collection of papers in S. Franklin and J. Shepard (eds.), *Byzantine Diplomacy* (Aldershot: Ashgate, 1992); Evangelos Chrysos, "Byzantine Diplomacy, A.D. 300–800: Means and Ends," in: J. Shepard and S. Franklin (eds.), *Byzantine Diplomacy: Papers from the Twenty-Fourth Spring Symposium of Byzantine Studies* (Aldershot: Variorium, 1992), 25–39; Jonathan Shepard, "Byzantine Diplomacy, A.D. 800–1204: Means and Ends," in: J. Shepard and S. Franklin (eds.), *Byzantine Diplomacy: Papers from the Twenty-Fourth Spring Symposium of Byzantine Studies* (Aldershot: Variorium, 1992), 41–71. I have also put together a model (or models?) of negotiation and confrontation between Byzantium and its neighbours that focuses (chronologically) on the tenth century and (geo-politically) on three different operational theatres: with the Arabs in the East, with the Bulgars in the West and with the Rus' and Patzinaks in the North: https://bit.ly/2AI9uwl.

the following centuries.[27] Finally, Syrianos' famous sentence in present tense τοῦτο δὲ ποιεῖ βελισάριος, "this is what Belisarius does," should rather be understood in the historic present tense without chronological implications, as the overwhelming majority of the examples from the distant classical past of Greece, Persia and Rome are also described by the author of the treatise in the same tense.[28] Rance added seven arguments that demonstrate the probability of Syrianos writing his *compendium* in the ninth century.

First, another of the author's famous sentences in the *On Strategy* that referred to the ambushes used by the Arabs had come under scrutiny already since Köchly and Rüstow's edition of the treatise: τὰς ἐνέδρας ποιοῦσι μέν καὶ οἱ σήμερον Ῥωμαῖοι τε καὶ Ἄραβες ("ambushes are used by both today's Romans and Arabs").[29] Historians have maintained for over a century that Syrianos' Ἄραβες were the empire's pre-Islamic Ghassanid allies, hence reinforcing the suggestion that the author was writing in the sixth century.[30] Lee and Shepard, Cosentino and Rance offered two counter-arguments to the established position: first, the marginal geo-political position of the empire's Arab/Beduin allies would not have qualified them for any mention in a military treatise of the sixth century; second, the late Antique and early Byzantine historians and chroniclers largely favoured the term Σαρακηνοί ["*sharqiyyin*," meaning "easterners"] to denote the Arabs over Ἄραβες, which is more common for the high period of Byzantine historiography.[31]

Moreover, Baldwin's emphasis on another passage in the *On Strategy* that seems to disprove the argument for the compilation of the treatise in the Justinianic period, is – actually – unfounded. Baldwin picked up on Syrianos' introduction of the four branches of battle tactics ("τὰ τῆς τακτικῆς μέρη") in the fourteenth chapter of the treatise, where the author explained, "I shall refrain from any treatment of elephants and chariots in the present work. For why should we still be discussing them, when even the terminology

27 Georgios Theotokis, *Byzantine Military Tactics in Syria and Mesopotamia in the Tenth Century, a Comparative Study* (Edinburgh: Edinburgh University Press, 2018), chapters 7 and 8.
28 Rance (2007), 709–11; Cosentino (2000), 263.
29 *On Strategy* in Dennis (1985/2008), chapter 40, 118.
30 Zuckerman (1990), 216; Dennis (1985/2008), 121 (n. 1); J. E. Wiita, "The Ethnika in Byzantine Military Treatises" (Unpublished PhD diss., University of Minnesota, Minneapolis, 1977), 373; Köchly and Rüstow (1853–1855), 38.
31 Rance (2007), 711–13; Cosentino (2000), 264–5; Lee and Shepard (1991), 26–7. Irfan Shahîd confirmed that the term Ἄραβες is, in fact, alien to the Byzantine historiography of the sixth century: *Byzantium and the Arabs in the Sixth Century* (Washington, DC: Dumbarton Oaks, 1995), 582–3.

for their tactical operations has become obsolete?"[32] On the surface, this may seem like a clear indication that the author was writing several generations after the Byzantine-Persian wars, since Baldwin, Lee and Shepard and Cosentino assumed that elephants played a prominent role in the wars between the two superpowers of the sixth century.[33] Yet Rance has demonstrated that although elephants frequently accompanied Sassanid armies on campaign for centuries, they had a very limited operational role, with the sole undisputed encounter of elephants by Roman troops in the battlefield witnessed at the Battle of Ganzak, in 591.[34] Rather, we should take Syrianos' remark about elephants and war-chariots as another antiquarianism that goes back to Asclepiodotos, Aelian, Arrian and, eventually, the Greek Stoic philosopher Poseidonios of Apameia's (c. 135 BC–c. 51 BC) description of the Seleucid army of the second century BC.[35]

Additionally, Rance included five observations that add to the general argument supporting the compilation of Syrianos' *compendium* in the (later) ninth century. First, he notes the description of the defensive structure of a military encampment in the *On Strategy*,[36] a military feature referred to in the tenth century as σκουταρῶμα (Latin "scutum"), that is not recorded in the sources of the sixth century, but it is well attested in the tenth and eleventh centuries.[37] In a similar fashion, he emphasizes that Syrianos' recommendation of the size of infantry shields of "no less than seven spithamai [c. 1,65 metres]" again has no parallels in the late Antique and early Byzantine sources, a size that is much more often documented in the tenth- and eleventh-century sources.[38] Rance also suggested that Syrianos' mentioning of armour for horses' hooves in the *On Strategy* may hint of a ninth-century compilation, since the one that our author describes resembles only another one from an unpublished Life of St. Philaretus the Younger (ca. 1020–76) (BHG 1513), an eleventh-century saint of Byzantine Calabria.[39] Furthermore, the fact that the editor/copyist of the codex *Ambrosianus graecus*

---

32 *On Strategy* in Dennis (1985/2008), chapter 14, 44.

33 Cosentino (2000), 265; Lee and Shepard (1991), 39; Baldwin (1988), 292–3.

34 P. Rance, "Elephants in Warfare in Late Antiquity," *Acta Antiqua Academiae Scientiarum Hungaricae* 43 (2003), 355–84.

35 Rance (2007), 716–19, with a rich bibliography in n. 55.

36 "[The soldiers should] fashion their spears and shields into a collective palisade, which will serve as a defensive perimeter and enclosure surrounding the army": *On Strategy* in Dennis (1985/2008), chapter 28, 86.

37 Rance (2007), 719–23, especially (n. 61, 62 and 67).

38 Rance (2007), 723–9; Georgios Theotokis, "Military Technology: Production and Use of Weapons," in: Y. Stouraitis (ed.), *A Companion to the Byzantine Culture of War, ca. 300–1204* (Leiden: Brill, 2018a), 458.

39 *On Strategy* in Dennis (1985/2008), chapter 17, 56; Rance (2007), 729–33.

119, which was commissioned sometime between 959 and early 960, chose not to paraphrase or edit the works by Syrianos, although he (linguistically) intervened in older texts to "update" the terminology for his contemporary readership, may suggest that "the editor . . . deemed it unnecessary or inappropriate to paraphrase a recently produced work."[40] Finally, Rance highlighted the absence of any majuscule/uncial errors in the manuscript witnesses to all three parts of Syrianos' compendium, which carries the implication that if it was written in the sixth century, it has had the remarkably good fortune to be transmitted through a series of "especially diligent copyists."[41]

Rance also emphasized the importance of a naval treatise like the *Naumachiae* in the *compendium* of Syrianos, compared to the predominantly "land-warfare" treatise of the sixth century *Strategikon*. If we consider that there was a significant upsurge of naval warfare around the middle of the ninth century (I will attempt to be more specific subsequently), it seems to me intrinsically plausible that a military *compendium* with a "naval element" would have made perfect sense for that period. This argument becomes stronger if we consider the famous "naval" Constitution 19, which, along with Constitutions 15 and 17 and other naval texts, was appended to the main text of Leo VI's *Tactical Constitutions* sometime between 904 and 912. This addition clearly reflects the rapidly deteriorating geo-political situation between the Empire and the Caliphate in the closing years of the ninth century and the growing threat of sea-based attacks that was becoming a major concern for Leo VI's administration.

We need to highlight two key arguments at this point before I try to pinpoint with greater accuracy the period of the compilation of Syrianos' *compendium*. First, what I wrote previously about the fact that the editor/copyist of the *codex Ambrosianus graecus 119* apparently did not paraphrase or edit the works by Syrianos, probably because he considered them recent scholarship on the subject of the art of war; this is important because it places Syrianos' *compendium* very close – chronologically – to Leo's *Tactical Constitutions*. On top of that, we have the complaint by the author of the *Tactical Constitutions*, at the beginning of the section "About Naval Warfare," that "we have found no regulations on this subject among the ancient tacticians."[42] Surely this comment on its own precludes the fact that many generations would have passed between the compilations of both works. Furthermore, Cosentino (following Lammert) suggested that Syrianos'

40 Rance (2007), 733–6.
41 Rance (2007), 736–7.
42 Dennis (2010), chapter 19, 502–3.

Naumachiae primarily reflects literary considerations, particularly that of the largely lost *compendium* of Aeneas Tacticus, an assumption that transformed Syrianos' naval treatise into the "literary heir" of a lost treatment of naval warfare which originally followed Aineias' *Poliorketika*.[43] Nevertheless, as Rance very poignantly suggested, "If Syrianus did have the good fortune to possess a naval treatise by Aineias, he appears to have been the only Greek, Roman or Byzantine writer ever to have seen a copy. Certainly Leo VI was less fortunate."[44] Therefore, Cosentino's and Lammert's argument does not sound very compelling to me, which only adds to the point about the close (chronological) relationship between Syrianos' and Leo's works. However, is it possible to narrow down even further the possible period of the compilation of Syrianos' *compendium*? I believe it is.

Dating the compendium and the geo-political background of the period

The basic strategic consideration that determined the empire's strategic thinking and planning for this period was to achieve a sort of equilibrium with its archenemy in the East, the Abbasid Caliphate.[45] Yet John Haldon aptly described the history of Byzantine warfare during the eighth and the ninth centuries as "a rather depressing one, for the empire often seems to have lost far more battles than it won."[46] Land warfare between the two great superpowers during the period of the so-called Amorian dynasty, which corresponded with the reigns of the emperors Michael II (reigned, 820–29), Theophilos (reigned, 829–42) and Michael III (842–67), was defined by two great pitched battles that occurred a quarter of a century apart.

Theophilos' disastrous defeat at the Battle of Anzen, on 22 July 838, was of significant political and strategic importance for the equilibrium of power in Asia Minor while also opening the way for the brutal sack of Ancyra (27 July) and Amorion (beginning of August). Out of – perhaps – 70,000 inhabitants that had flocked to Amorion in the weeks leading up to the attack, around half were massacred or sold as slaves by the Abbasids.[47] This was

---

43 Cosentino (2000), 260, 262, 279–80; Lammert (1940), 280 (n. 1), 281–2, 288.
44 Rance (2017), 322–3.
45 For the emperors and high officials, there was no succinct concept of "grand strategy," at least not in a way scholars would have understood it in the twentieth century, but rather a reaction to the socio-political events in the world that surrounded the empire: Theotokis (2018), 26–9.
46 John Haldon, *The Byzantine Wars* (Stroud: The History Press, 2009), 67.
47 Warren Treadgold, *A History of the Byzantine State and Society* (Stanford, CA: Stanford University Press, 1997), 441–2.

a devastating political and ideological setback for the "Amorian" dynasty, considering that Amorion was one of the empire's largest cities, the capital of the Anatolikon theme, and the one from which the imperial family's founder Michael II descended.

The defeat at Anzen and the sack of Amorion played an additional role in discrediting iconoclasm, as shortly after Theophilos' sudden death in 842, the veneration of icons was restored as part of the Triumph of Orthodoxy throughout the Empire.[48] Inevitably, these events had a deep impact on the Byzantine psyche, which is reflected in the numerous folk songs (Acritic songs) that have a survived since the eleventh century or – probably – even earlier. Examples include the *Song of Armouris* (Ἄσμα τοῦ Ἀρμούρη) that describes the efforts of a young Byzantine borderer to rescue his father from captivity, or the *Castle of the Beauty* (Κάστρο της Ωρ[α]ιάς) or *Castle of Mary* (Κάστρο της Μαρούς), a ballad about a fair maiden who fell from the battlements of her castle to her death to escape Muslim captivity.[49] These should be coupled with the veneration by the Church of the 42 martyrs of Amorion, the imperial officers that were captured in 838 and – allegedly – executed in Samarra seven years later for refusing to convert to Islam.[50] Finally, the middle of the ninth century was a period when the cultural and diplomatic activity between the Constantinopolitan and Baghdad courts increased exponentially,[51] which suggests a greater Byzantine awareness of Islam as a religious system and an ideology, to the point where Michael III asked Niketas Byzantios, a scholar from the entourage of Patriarch Photios,

---

48 Treadgold (1997), 441–2; Mark Whittow, *The Making of Byzantium, 600–1025* (Berkeley and Los Angeles, CA: University of California Press, 1996), 153–4.

49 For Medieval Greek poetry: Roderick Beaton, *Folk Poetry of Modern Greece* (Cambridge: Cambridge University Press, 2004). For the *Song of Armouris*: Georgios Thanopoulos, *Το Τραγούδι του Αρμούρη* [*The Song of Armouris*] (Saripolou: Athens, 1990). For the celebration of the sack of Amorion in the poetry of the Syrian convert to Islam Abū Tammām (796/807–850): A. J. Arberry, *Arabic Poetry: A Primer for Students* (Cambridge: Cambridge University Press, 1965), 50–62.

50 Kazhdan et al. (1991), 800–1. Kolia-Dermitzaki offers some interesting insights into the execution of the imperial officers as a valuable Abbasid propaganda exercise and a show of power: Athina Kolia-Dermitzaki, "The Execution of the Forty-two Martyrs of Amorion: Proposing an Interpretation," *Al-Masāq* 14 (2002), 141–62. However, Stouraitis argues that the story of the collective martyrdom of the 42 captives of Amorion is a mid-ninth-century Constantinopolitan invention for propagandistic reasons: Yannis Stouraitis, "Historicity, Agency, and Ideology: The Story of the Sack of Amorion Between Reality and Fiction," in: N. Tsivikis (ed.), *Byzantine Medieval Cities: Amorium and the Middle Byzantine Provincial Capitals* (Berlin: De Gruyter, forthcoming 2020–2021).

51 Paul Magdalino, "The Road to Baghdad in the Thought-World of Ninth-Century Byzantium," in: L. Brubaker (ed.), *Byzantium in the Ninth Century: Dead or Alive?* (London: Routledge, 1998), 195–214.

to compose a lengthy treatise that refuted the "new" religion.[52] However, I will talk more about the increasing Byzantine interest in Islam in the ninth century in the following.

Following the outbreak of civil war in the Caliphate, in 842, a combined force of some 15–20,000 men under the orders of the emir of Melitene, Umar al-Aqta (r. 830s–863), and the Abbasid governor of Tarsus broke into Anatolia through the Cilician Gates in late August 863, plundering and burning as they went.[53] Umar carried on in a northerly direction and succeeded in defeating an imperial army of around the same size, led by Michael III himself, in a bloody battle at an area known in Arab sources as Marj al-Usquf ("Bishop's Meadow"): a highland near Malakopeia, north of Nazianzos.[54] With Umar penetrating as far north as the Black Sea port of Amisos in the Armeniakon theme, it was the *Domestic of the Scholae*, Petronas, who was shadowing the invading force and managed to surround and defeat it on 3 September, at a location known as Poson (Πόσων), near the Lalakaon River, about 130 km southeast of Amisos.

The victory at Poson/Lalakaon encapsulates two key aspects of the Byzantine defence-in-depth strategy of the ninth century: first, the pincer movement designed to clear out the enemy columns by having several smaller neighbouring thematic forces converging in an area and, second, the degree of independence of the local commanders when it came to making decisions with adequate intelligence. Likewise, on a geo-political level, Poson/Lalakaon undoubtedly broke the power of the emirate of Melitene, leading the Byzantines to hail the outcome as a revenge for Amorion 25 years earlier.[55] Further Byzantine counterattacks against the heretic Paulicians in the region followed in the 870s.

The geo-political relations between the empire and the Arabs in the East that we just described fit very well with Cosentino's assessment of the most likely period for the compilation of Syrianos' *compendium*. The former brought forward some strong arguments that Syrianos would have been a contemporary of the events unfolding during Theophilos' times, while

---

52 Dirk Krausmüller, "Killing at God's Command: Niketas Byzantios' Polemic Against Islam and the Christian Tradition of Divinely Sanctioned Murder," *Al-Masāq* 16 (2004), 163–76; John Meyendorff, "Byzantine Views of Islam," *Dumbarton Oaks Papers* 18 (1964), 121–5.

53 What historians of the eastern Mediterranean would identify as a *razzia* was the kind of limited warfare verging on brigandage that avoided head-on confrontations and instead emphasized raiding and looting, usually of livestock: Theotokis (2018), chapter 2.

54 Haldon (2009), 87–9; George L. Huxley, "The Emperor Michael III and the Battle of Bishop's Meadow (A.D. 863)," *Greek, Roman, and Byzantine Studies* 16 (1975), 443–50.

55 Norman Tobias, Basil I, founder of the Macedonian Dynasty : a study of the political and military history of the Byzantine Empire in the Ninth century (Edwin Mellen: New York, 2007).

he – most likely – would have compiled his work shortly after the emperor's death in 842.[56] Nevertheless, even if we take the view that Syrianos did not have much technical knowledge or any experience of warfare, it is his decision to include a treatise on naval warfare in his *compendium* that can – most plausibly – be viewed as a response to recent/current developments, especially since a naval chapter thereafter became a standard component of Byzantine military *compendia* (i.e. "Constitution 19" in Leo's *Tactical Constitutions*). In my view, it is the significant upsurge in naval warfare after Basil I's usurpation of the imperial throne in 867 that can be linked with the decision to include the *Naumachiae*, a fact that could push the period for the compilation of Syrianos' work further forward to around the second half of the 870s.

Lounghis emphasized two critical points concerning the historical outline of the condition of the Byzantine navy in the eighth and – especially – the ninth centuries.[57] First, the major administrative reforms of the imperial navy during the first two emperors of the Macedonian dynasty, Basil I and Leo VI, that subjugated all the provincial naval forces to the needs of the new dynasty under a new officer, the *droungarios of the fleet*. Second, the ability of Byzantium to intervene in the West during the eighth and ninth centuries depended on the stability of the so-called "southern boundary," roughly defined as the sea-routes dominated by the islands of Cyprus, Crete, and the southern Aegean, a fact that clearly demonstrates the connection between geo-political events in Crete and Sicily/Italy.

Beginning with the latter point, it is fair to say that although the northern (Danubian) and eastern borders of the empire were protected by its land armies, hence the longer and more thorough treatment of their achievements in the primary sources, of equal strategic importance were the southern and the western borders that were safeguarded by various naval forces. Therefore, any gap in the naval boundaries of the empire in the Mediterranean Sea would have been equally ominous for the empire as a resurgent border *emir* in the Taurus Mountains or the loss of a strategic fortress town south of the Danube. Bearing that in mind, the restoration of the gap in the southern boundary that the Arabs had inflicted in the seventh century with the loss of

56 Cosentino (2000), 273–5.
57 Lounghis' is the most authoritative study to-date on the topic of Byzantine naval strategy in the Mediterranean Sea: Tilemachos Lounghis, *Byzantium in Eastern Mediterranean: Safeguarding East Roman Identity (407–1204)* (Nicosia: Cyprus Research Centre, 2010), especially chapters 3–4. Also outlined in: Tilemachos Lounghis, "The Byzantine War Navy and the West, Fifth to Twelfth Centuries," in: Georgios Theotokis and Aysel Yildiz (eds.), *A Military History of the Mediterranean Sea: Aspects of War, Diplomacy and Military Elites* (Leiden: Brill, 2018), 21–43 [especially pp. 22–6].

Cyprus, and with the more recent loss of Crete, should have been an urgent strategic priority for the Byzantine leadership compared to any expedition to the West (Italy and Sicily). However, as Lounghis emphasized, the imperial expeditions to the West throughout the ninth century "represented East Roman imperial predominance, and thus had absolute priority over the restoration of the southern boundary. Nevertheless, this priority did not hamper the successive plans . . . for the recovery of Cyprus and Crete."[58] Under Basil I, the empire apparently abandoned its ecumenical pretensions in the West in favour of defending its restricted dominion in Italy. This meant that, although the Muslim bases in Crete and southern Aegean were menacingly closer to the imperial capital than Palermo, Messina, or Bari, the founder of the "Macedonian" dynasty saw the need to keep the imperial flag flying in the West.

The strategic priority of neutralizing Cyprus before any conquest of Crete could take place is clearly reflected in Leo VI's *Tactical Constitutions*: "Now, as the barbarians are gathering together from Egypt, Syria, and Cilicia to campaign against the Romans, it is necessary for the fleet generals with their naval forces to occupy Cyprus before the barbarian ships can get together."[59] For that reason, it would certainly have looked paramount for Basil to capture the island of Cyprus, as this would have isolated Crete and deprived her of valuable supplies and reinforcements, while in Byzantine hands, it could have been used as a base to support land campaigns against Tarsus and northern Syria. The island's strategic importance in the eastern Mediterranean had already been recognized since the time of Justinian II (reigned 685–95 and 705–11), when the main base of the theme of Kibyrrhaeotae was established at Kibyrrha, opposite Cyprus on the southern coast of Asia Minor, a few years before 698.[60] Furthermore, two lead seals of two generals of the Kibyrrhaeotae (with the dignities of *spatharios* and *patrikios*, respectively)[61] that were found in Cyprus also hint at a large Byzantine naval presence in the waters between Asia Minor and Cyprus. Nevertheless, it was during Basil's reign that the empire regained possession of the island, although this was to prove ephemeral. The likeliest period of Byzantine rule was between the lull in the war against the Paulicians following the failure to take Melitene in 873 and the Arab retaking of the island in 880 or in 881, which again confirms the interdependency between different operational theatres of war.[62]

---

58 Lounghis (2010), 86–7.
59 Dennis (2010), XX. 612–13.
60 Lounghis (2010), 88–91.
61 Bury (1911), 22.
62 Tobias (2007), 128.

The only time in the history of Byzantine naval affairs in the eastern Mediterranean that the strategic goal of conquering Cyprus was overshadowed by another more pressing geo-political development was the period following the "Spaniard" Arab conquest of Crete during the reign of Michael II (820–29). The Byzantines reacted swiftly to the sudden and unexpected loss of this strategic island by dispatching three expeditions to reclaim it before the death of Michael II in October 829, but they all failed miserably. Surprisingly, the only expedition launched thereafter against the Cretan Arabs until the reign of Leo VI was the one led by the *magistros* and *logothetes tou dromou* Theoktistos in 843, which only achieved short-lived success.

Undoubtedly, the loss of Crete shifted the strategic makeup of the eastern Mediterranean, escalating the naval activity in the Aegean Sea for the following century and a half. Yet we should not construe these raids by the Arabs from Crete as mindless opportunistic pirate raids but rather as meticulously planned military expeditions that aimed either at booty or at the permanent conquest of an island.[63] Around 839, they inflicted a major defeat on a Byzantine fleet off Thasos in the northern Aegean, and around 860, they raided the Cyclades, reaching as far north as the Dardanelles. Nasr's raid on the town of Methymna in Lesbos in 867 also became famous through the *Life of Saint Theoktiste of Lesbos*. In the third quarter of the century, permanent Muslim occupation was witnessed for the islands of Karpathos, to the south of Rhodes; of Cos, between Rhodes and Samos; of Naxos, the biggest of the Cycladic islands in the southern Aegean, of Paros; and of Aegina in the Saronic Gulf.[64]

This increasing naval activity in the Aegean Sea forced successive imperial governments to revise the distribution of naval forces in their "southern boundary" in an effort to safeguard the critical navigational routes that crossed the western and eastern coasts of Crete. Under the "Amorian" emperors, we see the disappearance of the general of the Kibyrrhaeotae,[65] while the fleet of the newly established (probably shortly after 843)[66] *theme of the Aegean Sea* was reported operating in the southern Aegean but with mixed results, as attested in the *Lives of Saints Peter of Argos* and *Euthymius and Theodore of Cythera*.[67] On top of that, Michael III dispatched a strong fleet against Abbasid Egypt in 852/53 (repeated in 859), which sacked

63 Vasilios Christides, "The Raids of the Moslems of Crete in the Aegean Sea, Piracy and Conquest," *Byzantion* 51 (1981), 76–111.

64 Tobias (2007), 124–27; Pryor (2006), 47; Christides (1981), 82–88.

65 A number of seals show that a subordinate officer, a *turmarch* (of Pamphylia), probably replaced the general of the Kibyrrhaeotae: Lounghis (2010), 96 (n. 717).

66 Lounghis (2018), 24.

67 Christides (1981), 87–8.

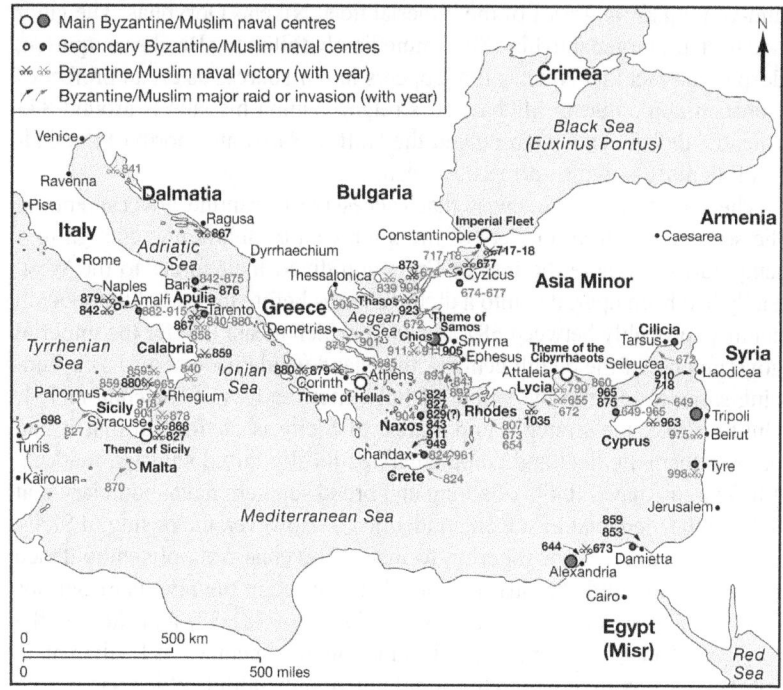

Figure 1.1 Map of the Mediterranean

Damietta; apparently, the Byzantine leadership had – finally – grasped the fact that Egypt was also critical as a supply base for the Cretan naval activity in the eastern Mediterranean.[68]

Things improved dramatically for the empire during Basil I's reign, although victories over the Cretan Arabs began to show results only in the second half of the 870s.[69] The sources attest to a naval victory by the general of the *theme of Hellas* (est. around 687), a certain Oiniates, over a relatively small fleet from Tarsus that was raiding Euripos (modern Chalkida) in Euboea, either around 875 or shortly after 883.[70] Then, following a Cretan naval raid against Methone, Patras and Corinth in the Peloponnesus

---

68 Christides (1981), 92.
69 Tobias (2007), 124–7; Pryor (2006), 61; Christides (1981), 92–3.
70 Pryor (2006), 62; Christides (1981), 93.

around 879, the Arabs were annihilated in the Gulf of Corinth by the up-and-coming *droungarios* of the imperial fleet, Niketas Ooryphas. The latter had been promoted into his office immediately following Basil's usurpation, despite the fact that Niketas first appears in our sources as urban prefect of Constantinople during Michael III's reign, gaining his laurels around 873 when he defeated a Cretan fleet at the Gulf of Saros, just north of the Gallipoli Peninsula in the northern Aegean.

The fact remains, however, that successive Byzantine governments in the second and third quarters of the ninth century felt strong enough to – temporarily – ignore the loss of Crete and divert their forces to the West. Sicily had been upgraded into a theme already before the end of the seventh century (probably between 687 and 695), which meant that for the imperial governments of the eighth century, the island would have served as a stepping stone to reclaim the whole of Italy after the loss of Ravenna in 751. Unlike Crete, the strategic importance of Sicily is obvious in that it had its own thematic fleet and complement of locally raised soldiers, marking "the extreme naval limits of a long and broad southern naval boundary that defined the medieval East Roman identity."[71] However, the raising of Sicily to a rank similar, if not superior, to that of Ravenna certainly emboldened its generals towards "centrifugal acts," as we see in the revolts of Sergios (in 717/18), Antiochos (in 764/65), Elpidios (in 781/82) and, finally, the *turmarch* Ephemios (in 827); this is important to remember, as I will explain subsequently, with regard to the appointment of "faithful" officers in charge of an upgraded imperial fleet by the new "Macedonian" dynasty. Moreover, it is understood that the eventual loss of Sicily to the "African" Arabs came not only as a devastating blow to the empire's prestige, but it also dismantled its (unofficial) "western [naval] boundary."[72] As a direct result of that, we see the Sicilian fleet retreating to Calabria sometime in the middle of the ninth century.[73]

When they were able, the Byzantines dispatched substantial fleets to the West, such as the one under Alexios Musele in 838. Musele was the son-in-law of emperor Theophilos (829–842) and was sent to reverse the Arab expansion in Sicily, bringing with him some 4,000 elite troops that were carried to Sicily by the newly established imperial fleet (βασιλικὸν

---

71 Lounghis (2010), 117–18. See also: Lounghis (2018), 29–31.

72 Lounghis (2010), 120–1.

73 Agostino Pertusi, "Il 'thema' di Calabria: Sua formazzione, lotte per la sopravivenza. Società a clero di fronte a Bisanzio e a Roma," in: *Byzantino-Sicula II: Miscellanea di scritti in memoria di Giuseppe Rossi Taibbi* (Palermo: Istituto siciliano di studi bizantini e neoellenici, 1975), 425–43 [here: 428].

πλώιμον).[74] That was to no avail, as the Sicilian Arabs renewed their attacks and, worst of all, they took Messina (in 842), Brindisi (in 838), and Taranto (in 839), despite the effort of a Venetian fleet of 60 *naves* sent at imperial request to relieve Taranto in 840. A sizeable imperial fleet of 300 suffered another defeat in 859, resulting in the Arab conquest of the key Sicilian fortress of Enna (Castrogiovanni), thus confirming to the eyes of Michael III's government that the loss of Sicily was irreversible.

Basil I's first act as emperor in securing the frontiers of the empire was to dispatch a powerful fleet under the *patrikios* and *droungarios of the fleet* Niketas Ooryphas for a campaign to the West. The fleet first saw action in Dalmatia, in 868, where the Sicilian Arabs had renewed their attacks since 858, coming to the relief of Ragusa, and news of the approach of the imperial fleet forced the Arabs to end their long siege and to hurry back to Italy.[75] Lounghis made a significant point regarding Basil's policy in the West during his first few years on the throne: the Byzantines abandoned Sicily in favour of southern Italy only after the siege of Arab-held Bari under the King of Italy and Holy Roman Emperor Louis II (reigned 855–75), which was assisted by the imperial fleet under Ooryphas, succeeded in expelling the Arabs in 871.[76] This point is reinforced by the appearance of an imperial fleet at Otranto in 873, while another fleet managed to reclaim Bari from the Germans in 876; this was more of a power shift than a strategic retreat to Italy, which was wrapped up with the Byzantine conquest of the last Arab-held city in Italy, Taranto, in 880. In the same year, when an Aghlabid fleet raided Kephalonia and Zakynthos in the Ionian Sea, Basil dispatched a fleet under the *patrikios* and *droungarios of the fleet* Naser (Nasr), who destroyed them off the coast of western Greece after cleverly using the bold tactic of night attack, as recommended in Leo's "naval constitution."[77]

It is during the early years of Basil I's reign that we notice the significant upgrade of the *droungarios of the fleet*, who enjoyed a much higher position and prestige than during the previous period of the "Amorians," as we see in the so-called *Taktikon Uspensky* (843) and in the so-called *Klētorologion of Philotheos* (899).[78] Basil's strengthening of the imperial fleet, which the Continuators of Theophanes report being permanently moored in the capital during his reign, must have been carried out by the subordination of smaller naval units, for example, the recently revived theme of the Kibyrrhaeotae

---

74 Lounghis (2010), 124–7.
75 Perhaps it was at this time that the *Archondate of Dalmatia* was upgraded into a theme: Tobias (2007), 155.
76 Lounghis (2010), 132.
77 Dennis (2010), XIX. 57, 526–7.
78 Lounghis (2018), 25; Lounghis (2010), 135, 138–9.

that had been absent from the naval conflicts with the Arabs in the Mediterranean since the 820s.[79]

According to Lounghis, there is a critical correlation between the attempts made by the first two "Macedonian" emperors to centralize the naval forces of the empire under the command of the *droungarios of the fleet* in Constantinople and a passage in the *De Administrando Imperio* (compiled between 948–52), attributed to Basil's grandson Constantine VII (reigned 913–59).[80] In the aforementioned passage, the author pays great attention to the appointment of "trusted" naval officers in charge of the Mardaites of southern Asia Minor and the theme of Kibyrrhaeotae, clearly stressing the dynasty's preference for officers of lower social origins over the high-ranking noblemen who had the power and prestige to defy them. A typical case is that of Eustathios Argyros, who first appeared during the outbreak of war with Bulgaria in 894 under the overall command of Nikephoros Phokas the Elder, another "loyal" and "reliable" army general repeatedly called τὸν ἡμέτερον στρατηγόν ("our general") in Leo's *Tactical Constitutions*.[81] When Leo VI sent a fleet under Eustathios to aid Taormina in Sicily in 902, and following his return to Constantinople after the city's fall to the Muslims, Eustathios and Constantine Karamallos, Taormina's garrison commander, were accused of negligence and even high treason. However, Lounghis emphasized the bias of contemporary sources reporting on the aforementioned events, including the – alleged – "treachery" of another admiral, Adrianos, concerning the loss of Syracuse in 878. Sources hostile to the new dynasty of the "Macedonians" highlighted the inability and outright treachery of these admirals, while those that favoured the new regime simply whitewashed or altogether failed to mention the details behind these disasters.[82]

To reiterate about the two critical points I outlined at the beginning of this section concerning the historical outline of the Byzantine navy in the ninth century: first, I have clearly shown that the empire's geo-political stability depended on the cohesion of the so-called "southern naval boundary" that included the islands of Cyprus, Crete, and Sicily. Furthermore, I have described how it was after Basil I's seizure of the throne in 867 that

79 I. Ševčenko (ed. and trans.), *Chronographiae Quae Theophanis Continuati Nomine Fertur Liber Quo Vita Basilii Imperatoris Amplectitur* (Berlin: De Gruyter, 2011), 234–7; Lounghis (2010), 137.

80 Constantine Porphyrogennetos, *De Administrando Imperio* (Greek text), G. Moravcsik (ed.) and R. J. H. Jenkins (trans.) (Washington, DC: Dumbarton Oaks, 1985), ch. 50, 240–5.

81 Dennis (2010), XI. 202–3; XV. 366–7; XVII. 418–19.

82 Lounghis (2010), 132–5.

the balance of sea power in the Eastern Mediterranean tilted decisively in favour of the Byzantines, even if it might not have seemed so at the time. The fact remains, however, that Emperor Basil's new western policy involving southern Italy instead of Sicily was radically different from that of his "Amorian" predecessors, and the operational theatre of Italy would always take precedence in the mind of Basil over Cyprus or Crete. Attempts to reclaim these two islands would only be made once the new "Macedonian" dynasty felt strong enough to undertake such a campaign, but not earlier than 873 and 911, respectively. Finally, the major administrative reforms of the imperial navy that subjugated all the provincial naval forces, including the re-fitted fleet of the Kibyrrhaeotae, to the needs of the new dynasty under the *droungarios of the fleet*, combined with the meticulous imperial attention paid to the appointment of officers faithful to the new regime, reveal the decisive (or desperate?) attempts of the "Macedonians" to secure the reins of power.

Therefore, I believe that Syrianos' decision to include a treatise on naval warfare in his *compendium* fits much better into the geo-political environment of the second half of Basil I's reign, roughly between 875 and 886, than the period suggested by Cosentino following the death of Theophilos in 842. This argument grows stronger considering that a naval chapter thereafter became a standard component of Byzantine military *compendia*, like the famous "Constitution 19" in Leo's *Tactical Constitutions*, a military manual that also grew out of the late ninth-century cultural milieu of Christian-Muslim conflict to form an integral part of Emperor Leo's scheme of setting the empire's "military administration" on a sound footing by introducing imperial legislation to be accepted as instruction rather than suggestion.[83]

A note on the sources

Modern historians have proposed that Syrianos made selective reworking of earlier sources from the late Hellenistic sub-genre of military literature, some of which they have been able to identify. For example, his discussion on tactics in the *On Strategy* is – largely – drawn from Aelian, a Greek living in Rome in the early second century AD who based his *Tactical Theory* on the art of war developed in the late Hellenistic period, with the

83 Meredith L. D. Riedel, *Leo VI and the Transformation of Byzantine Christian Identity: Writings of an Unexpected Emperor* (Cambridge: Cambridge University Press, 2018), chapter 2; John F. Haldon, *A Critical Commentary on the Taktika of Leo VI* (Washington, DC: Dumbarton Oaks, 2014), 80–7; P. Magdalino, "The Non-Juridical Legislation of the Emperor Leo VI," in: S. Troianos (ed.), *Analecta Atheniensia ad ius Byzantinum spectantia I* (Athens: Sakkoulas Publishers, 1997), 169–82.

Macedonian phalanx as his model.[84] The *On Strategy*'s "tactical" chapters comply with the general order in the *Tactical Theory* although, as Zuckerman notes, Syrianos chose to modify the arrangement of Aelian's definitions while, in some cases, he disregarded some of the topics in the *Tactical Theory*, or he included others that were entirely his own, like the chapter on river crossings (*On Strategy*, chapter 19) that he introduced with the following justification: "Since journeys are made not only on dry land but also across water, it is necessary to talk about crossing rivers." Likewise, his analysis of fortifications and signal fires in the *On Strategy* prompted some historians to speculate that he drew on the *Poliorketika* of Philo of Byzantium (ca. 200 BC) and, perhaps, the lost books of Aeneas Tacticus (ca. mid-fourth century BC).[85] Finally, Syrianos also overtly criticizes the practicality of Apollodoros of Damascus' (2nd c. AD) floating bridge in crossing rivers.[86]

On the other hand, while Aelian remains an anonymous source in the *compendium*, Syrianos openly notes in the *Rhetorica Militaris* (chapter 3.2–4) that he is deliberately departing from Hermogenes in not formulating opposing arguments to war. Hermogenes of Tarsus (c. AD160–230) was, perhaps, the most influential rhetorical theorist of Late Antiquity, during the time of the so-called Second Sophistic[87] (first three centuries of the Common Era), when epideictic oratory (a type of persuasive speech designed primarily for rhetorical effect and display) had become a major literary force in the eastern Mediterranean. As basic handbooks on Greek rhetorical theory proliferated in the early sixth century, amongst the most authoritative in the field that were taught as separate "preliminary exercises," or *progymnasmata*, were Aphthonius' *Progymnasmata* (later fourth century), Hermogenes' *Peri staseon* ("On Issues") and *Peri ideon* ("On Ideas"), and Menander of Laodicea's epideictic treatises (also known as Menander Rhetor; late third century).[88] These works would have been taught at several levels of the

---

84 Zuckerman considers in detail Syrianos' word-for-word quotations from Aelian in the *On Strategy*. Zuckerman (1990), 217–19. Moreover, the same author dismisses Syrianos' reading of Asclepiodotos and Arrian.

85 This view is not universally accepted. See the detailed footnote in Rance (2007), 704 (n. 9). See also: Rance (2017), especially: 314–25.

86 *On Strategy* in Dennis (1985/2008), chapter 19, 62.

87 Joy Connolly, "The New World Order: Greek Rhetoric in Rome," in: Ian Worthington (ed.), *A Companion to Greek Rhetoric* (London: Blackwell, 2007), 159–61; Thomas Conley, *Rhetoric in the European Tradition* (Chicago, IL: The University of Chicago Press, 1990), 59–63.

88 E. Jeffreys, "Rhetoric," in: *Oxford Handbook of Byzantine Studies* (Oxford: Oxford University Press, 2009), 828–33; E. Jeffreys, "Rhetoric in Byzantium," in: Ian Worthington (ed.), *A Companion to Greek Rhetoric* (London: Blackwell, 2007), 166–84 [especially: 168–71]. For the life and works of Aphthonius, Hermogenes, and Menander Ruth Webb,

regular education in Byzantium, the *enkyklios paideia*,[89] to the extent that even writers such as the late eleventh-century Kekaumenos, a man of provincial military background, would have been aware of some basic *progymnasmata*.[90] Therefore, for students whose ambition would have been to earn a career at the higher levels of the state bureaucracy, proficiency in this kind of literary education would have been a prerequisite; Syrianos would have been no exception.

To support the aforementioned point about Syrianos' advanced education in rhetoric, Zuckerman highlights the language of the author in the *On Strategy* concerning the reasons he was writing his work:

> A phalanx is a formation of armed men designed to hold off the enemy. It may assume a variety of shapes: the circle, the lozenge, the rhomboid, the wedge . . . and many others which we shall not bother to discuss in this work, since very few people nowadays have any practical knowledge of tactics.[91]

The language of most of the authors of military treatises, including Syrianos, vividly portrays their frustration and intense concern over the future of their polities, which is translated into stereotypic rhetorical and philological models that glorify the past and lament their own times. Mindful and anxious that they live in a period of intense socio-political, ideological, and military upheaval, it is a common trait for the authors of these manuals to blame their contemporaries not just for not consulting previous treatises on military matters but also for completely ignoring the study of the science of war.[92] Moreover, although Syrianos felt the need to add more definitions

---

"Aphthonius," in: *Oxford Dictionary of Late Antiquity* (Oxford: Oxford University Press, 2018), 94; Malcolm Heath, "Hermogenes and the Hermogenean Corpus in Late Antiquity," in: *Oxford Dictionary of Late Antiquity* (Oxford: Oxford University Press, 2018), 714; Malcolm Heath, "Menander Rhetor," in: *Oxford Dictionary of Late Antiquity* (Oxford: Oxford University Press, 2018), 1003; George A. Kennedy (ed. and trans.), *Progymnasmata, Greek Textbooks of Prose Composition and Rhetoric* (Atlanta, GA: Society of Biblical Literature, 2003); Hugo Rabe and George A. Kennedy (ed. and trans.), *Invention and Method in Greek Rhetorical Theory: Two Rhetorical Treatises from the Hermogenic Corpus* (Atlanta, GA: Society of Biblical Literature, 2005); Conley (1990), 53–9.

89 A. Markopoulos, "Education," in: *Oxford Handbook of Byzantine Studies* (Oxford: Oxford University Press, 2009), 785–95.

90 Jeffreys (2008), 830.

91 *On Strategy* in Dennis (1985/2008), chapter 15, 46.

92 Georgios Theotokis and Aysel Yildiz, "Diffusion of Military Knowledge in the 17th Century Ottoman Empire: The Case of Esirî Hasan Ağa's 'Advices to Commanders and Soldiers'," *Mediterranean Chronicle* 8 (2018), 105–42 [here: 122–3]; T. G. Kolias, "Η

in his "tactical" chapters of the *On Strategy*, he did not feel the need to explain himself when writing about the "other stylistic forms" that the general should have been able to use in his exhortation speech to the troops (*Rhetorica Militaris*, 51). Therefore, not only was Syrianos well acquainted with Hermogenes' doctrines on delivering exhortation speeches, he would also have assumed that his audience would have been too fully aware of Hermogenes' writings on the forms of rhetorical style for him to repeat it in any detail.[93]

Finally, the true quality of the *Rhetorica Militaris* compared to the Late Antique *progymnasmata* can be summed up in the practical value of Syrianos' treatise as a textbook of "military rhetoric." Zuckerman identified a critical distinction between the *Rhetorica Militaris* and the *progymnasmata* in the sense that the former "filtered out" most of the examples of myths, historical anecdotes, gnomic sayings, or any other dry rhetorical elements, favouring, instead, the practical element of the material at the general's disposal:[94]

> So we will talk about the other parts of the speech, how each of them is used, but also about the differences between them. We will do this not only with a didactic exposition,[95] but also in a practical way, through examples, both for the sake of clarity, but also to show the abundance of similar [examples/elements].[96]

To give an example of Syrianos' departure from the Late Antique rhetorical handbooks and the challenging task of adapting the earlier material for his own main character – the general – we can compare an extract from the *Rhetorica Militaris* with chapter 4, "On War and Peace," of the *On Invention*,[97] a work on the parts of a rhetorical speech which, along with the "On Method," was combined sometime in fifth- or sixth-century Byzantium with the two authentic works by Hermogenes and Aphthonius' *Progymnasmata* to form a comprehensive and authoritative rhetorical corpus:

> Similarly, if we introduce a motion to go to war with someone or to end a war, we shall use *prokatastasis* as follows. If we are introducing a

πολεμική τακτική των βυζαντινών: θεωρία και πράξη" [The Military Tactics of the Byzantines: Theory and Practice], in: N. Oikonomides (ed.), *Byzantium at War (9th–12th Century)* (Athens: National Research Foundation, 1997), 153–64.
93 Zuckerman (1990), 219–20.
94 Zuckerman (1990), 221–2.
95 διδασκαλικῶς: in a didactic manner.
96 RM, 8.1.
97 Rabe and Kennedy (2005), xiii–xix.

motion to go to war with someone, we shall run over earlier complaints and say that "we ought to have gone to war with these people long ago, for they are enemies and have committed many other wrongs against us before these," then coming to what has now happened. . . . If, on the other hand, we are for putting an end to a war, the *prokatastasis* of the *diegesis* will be that "not even in the first place should we have set this war in motion," and we shall use historical reasons if we have any. . . . But if we have no support from history, the *prokatastasis* will contain an attack on the war, to the effect that "we should not have raised this war in the first place, abandoning peace, for war is a difficult thing and unpleasant," listing the evils in it, "and peace is good," listing the good things in it.[98]

I do not ignore that Hermogenes, and other rhetoricians before and after him, argue that pragmatism is a situation in which you can talk about future issues, but at the same time to compose the appropriate counter-arguments from the exact same premises. 3. We, however, who write about war according to pragmatism, will not construct opposite arguments (and how could we?), but will deal only with exhortations to war, which is one of the two parts of the war-peace question. For that reason, we have disregarded any mention of the refutation [of war].[99]

Syrianos emphasizes that he is deliberately deviating from Hermogenes in not formulating opposing arguments, since when a general exhorts to war, no consideration is given to the opposing point of view, that of peace. Therefore, it becomes clear that his aim was not to produce yet another rhetorical guide on deliberating war and peace in an Ancient Greek or Roman *agorá* but rather to deliver an applied rhetorical handbook for a general.

The manuscript tradition

The first of the earliest surviving family of manuscripts containing the *Rhetorica Militaris* (fs. 218ʳ–232ᵛ) is the codex **Mediceo-Laurentianus graecus, 55.4** (LV.4).[100] This is the original, or a copy,[101] of a voluminous collection of 16 Hellenistic, Late Roman, and Byzantine military treatises that included the works of Asclepiodotos, Aeneas Tacticus, Onasander, and

---

98 Rabe and Kennedy (2005), 42–5.

99 RM, 3.2–3.

100 Imma Eramo, *Siriano Discorsi di Guerra* (Bari: Dedalo, 2010), 24–5; Alphonse Dain, "Les Stratégistes Byzantins," *Travaux et Mémoires* 2 (1967), 382–5.

101 *Taktika*, in Dennis (2010), x. Arguments against it being a "copy": Rance (2017), 302–7 (with extensive bibliography).

Leo VI and Constantine VII[102] and which was commissioned in the imperial *scriptorium*[103] under the auspices of Emperor Constantine VII sometime between 950 and 955.[104]

The *Laurentianus* remained in Constantinople until the dispersal of the imperial library during/after the Fourth Crusade, before it found itself in the ownership of Demetrios Lascaris-Leontaris (d. 1431), an important Byzantine statesman and military leader of the period serving under the emperors Manuel II Palaiologos (r. 1391–1425) and John VIII Palaiologos (r. 1425–1448).[105] In 1491, it passed into the ownership of the Medici family in Florence, for whom the noted Greek Renaissance scholar Janus Lascaris was working. As a librarian to Lorenzo de Medici (sole ruler of Florence, 1478–92), Janus toured the Levant (1489–92), and his records of the manuscripts he sought, examined, or purchased to bring back to Florence are of immense value for the history of learning.[106] The *Laurentianus* was stored in the Medici-built Laurentian Library (*Biblioteca Medicea Laurenziana*) of Florence shortly after 1521.[107]

Dain identified 29 copies that are (directly or indirectly) dependent on the *Laurentianus*.[108] The oldest and most famous of these is the sixteenth-century **Parisinus graecus 2522**,[109] where the *Rhetorica Militaris* can be found in fs. 78^r–110^v and which Köchly used for his 1855–56 edition. It was probably copied either in Rome or in Florence between 1490 and 1530,[110] then passed into the *Bibliotheca Colbertina*, the library of about 20,000 volumes that was owned successively by Jean Baptiste Colbert de Torcy; Jacques Nicolas Colbert, Archbishop of Rouen (1655–1707); and Charles Eleonor Colbert, Comte de Seignely (d. 1747), before being purchased by the library of the King of France in Paris in 1728.

---

102 On the structure of the codex: Eramo (2010), 24; Dain (1967), 383.

103 Jean Irigoin, "Pour une ètude des centres de copie byzantins," *Scriptorium* 13 (1959), 178–81.

104 Haldon (2014), 55; Dennis (2010), x; Dennis (2008), 5. See also the cited bibliography in Rance (2017), 302–3 (n. 35).

105 Eramo (2010), 24.

106 Rance (2017), 305; Graham Speake, "Janus Lascaris' Visit to Mount Athos in 1491," *Greek, Roman and Byzantine Studies* 34 (1993), 325–30; J. Whittaker, "Janus Laskaris at the court of Charles V," *Thesaurismata* 14 (1977), 76–109.

107 See extensive bibliography in Rance (2017), 305 (n. 43).

108 Dain (1967), 382; Alphonse Dain, *La collection florentine des tacticiens grecs, essai sur une entreprise philologique de la renaissance* (Paris: Les Belles Lettres, 1940).

109 Eramo (2010), 25–6; Karaple (2010), 40; Alphonse Dain, "Le Parisinus gr. 2522," *Revue de Philologie* 15 (1941), 21–8; Dain (1940), 33, 43 (n. 2).

110 The BnF catalogue gives the date of copying as 1490–1530: https://gallica.bnf.fr/ark:/12148/btv1b107218513 [last accessed: 28.10.2020].

Another well-known copy is the **Bernensis 97**,[111] which includes the *Rhetorica Militaris* in fs. 153^r–192^r. Copied in Florence in the sixteenth century, it passed first into the library of Pierre Daniel of Orleans, (born 1531, Orléans–died 1604, Paris), a French lawyer, philologist and scholar, and later into that of Jacques Bongars,[112] (born 1554, Orléans–died 1612, Paris), a French diplomat and classical scholar who compiled the *Gesta Dei per Francos*, a collection of contemporary accounts of the Crusades. Following the death of Bongars, in 1612, the Library of Bern purchased the *Bernensis*. The **Parisinus graecus 2446**,[113] though – strictly speaking – is a secondary copy of the *Bernensis* rather than a direct apograph of the *Laurentianus*; it dates to the seventeenth century and contains the *Rhetorica Militaris* in fs. 68^r–84^r.

Finally, a smaller (20.4 × 13 cm) copy of the *Laurentianus*, which can be dated with certainty to the seventeenth century, is the **Barberinianus graecus 59**.[114] Lukas Holste copied this codex in Florence before it was passed into the Barberini Library in Rome, and it was moved once again in 1902, when the Vatican Library purchased the Barberini Library, which had rivalled it in importance in the seventeenth century. As Eramo rightly pointed out, Holste's hypothesis of the common authorship of the *On Strategy* and the *Rhetorica Militaris* determined his placing of the treatises in succession within the codex, with the former contained in fs. 26^r–84^v and the latter in fs. 86^r–111^v.

A second surviving family of manuscripts is the codex **Ambrosianus B 119 sup. (139)**,[115] a parchment manuscript consisting of 347 folios, 29.5 × 22.5 cm, with 31 lines to a page. Mazzucchi convincingly argued that it was the influential courtier Basil the *parakoimomenos* who commissioned the *Ambrosianus*, sometime between 959 and early 960, to promote his candidacy for the imperial campaign to reclaim Crete from the Arabs in 960–61.[116] The *Ambrosianus* is, undoubtedly, independent from the *Laurentianus*, thus pointing to a common ancestor that was already missing its last folio, since they both end abruptly.[117] More significantly, however, the importance of

111 Eramo (2010), 26; Dain (1940), 36–42. The codex was first presented by: H. Köchly, *De scriptorum militarium Graecorum codice Bernensi dissertatio* (Zürich, 1854).
112 https://bit.ly/2BOkuJ5 [last accessed: 7.7.2020].
113 Eramo (2010), 26–7.
114 Eramo (2010), 27.
115 Haldon (2014), 56; Eramo (2010), 27–8; Rance (2007), 733–6; Dain (1967), 385.
116 C. M. Mazzucchi, "Dagli anni di Basilio Parakimomenos (cod. Ambr. B 119 sup.)," *Aevum* 52 (1978), 267–316 [here: 293, 303–5]; Cosentino (2000), 243–6.
117 Eramo (2010), 29–31; Karaple (2010), 43; Dain (1940), 62, 66; T. Erck, "Anonymi Byzantini Peri Strategikes" (Unpublished PhD diss., University of Illinois, Urbana-Champaign, 1937), 10–14.

28 *Introduction*

the *Ambrosianus* lies in the fact that it is the only manuscript to contain all three extant sections of the *compendium* attributed to Syrianos: the *On Strategy* (only chapters 15–33 in fs. 6ʳ–17ᵛ), the *Rhetorica Militaris* [only the final part, from chapter 41.2 (acc. Köchly) in fs. 135ʳ–140ᵛ], and the *Naumachiae* (fs. 333ʳ–338ᵛ). The few things we know about the history of the codex put it in the ownership of Gian Vincenzo Pinelli (1535–1601), an Italian humanist born in Naples who was known during his time as having perhaps the best private library in Italy in the second half of the sixteenth century.[118] The *Biblioteca Ambrosiana* in Milan purchased Pinelli's collection of manuscripts after his death in 1608. Pinelli also commissioned a copy of the *Ambrosianus* sometime in the late sixteenth century, a codex known today as ***Marcianus graecus 976.1***,[119] which ended up in the Marciana Library in Venice in 1713.

Part B: the contents of the work

The history of exhortation and exhortative speeches

In his *Histories* (2nd c. BC), Polybius classified speeches in ancient Greek and Roman historiography into three categories:

> But to convince those also who are disposed to champion him I must speak of the principle on which he [author] composes public speeches, harangues to soldiers, the discourses of ambassadors, and, in a word, all utterances of the kind, which, as it were, sum up events and hold the whole history together.[120]

From this, we accept that speeches by generals to their army were of two kinds. First, there is the speech – deliberative or exhortative – delivered at a place resembling an assembly place, like standing or sitting in a horseshoe facing the speaker. Another type is the battle exhortation, allegedly delivered to the army when drawn up in battle formation or during the battle. The key point to differentiate between the two is timing; hence, a rough division into pre-battle and battle speeches should suffice for the purposes of this

---

118 Marcella Grendler, "A Greek Collection in Padua: The Library of Gian Vincenzo Pinelli (1535–1601)," *Renaissance Quarterly* 33 (1980), 386–416.
119 Eramo (2010), 28–9.
120 [Polybius, *Histories*, 12.25.a3] "ἵνα δὲ καὶ τοὺς φιλοτιμότερον διακειμένους μεταπείσωμεν, ῥητέον ἂν εἴη περὶ τῆς αἱρέσεως αὐτοῦ καὶ μελέτης τῆς κατὰ τὰς δημηγορίας καὶ τὰς παρακλήσεις, ἔτι δὲ τοὺς πρεσβευτικοὺς λόγους, καὶ συλλήβδην πᾶν τὸ τοιοῦτο γένος, ἃ σχεδὸν ὡς εἰ κεφάλαια τῶν πράξεών ἐστι καὶ συνέχει τὴν ὅλην ἱστορίαν."

study. Finally, the terminology used by ancient Greek authors to indicate these kinds of speeches includes the nouns δημηγορία (=a speech in the public assembly),[121] παραίνεσις (=exhortation, address),[122] and παράκλησις (=a calling to one's aid and/or an exhortation).[123] On top of that, the title of our *Δημηγορίαι Προτρεπτικαί πρός Ανδρείαν* (i.e. the Greek title of the *Rhetorica Militaris*) translates as "exhortative/encouraging (Greek: προτροπή)[124] public speeches to induce courage."

Exhortation speeches have as their archetype the (pre-)battle speeches in Homer's *Iliad*, to which historiography owes not just the historian's acknowledgement of why one side defeated the other but also the appearance of the main motifs of the exhortation in a speech, like the value of giving one's life for the country, living up to the reputation of the ancestors, and so on, as I will explain subsequently.[125] Homer is also famous for his ἐπιπώλησις (=going around), or "review of the troops" in the *Iliad*, in which Agamemnon passes along the Achaeans addressing a succession of pre-battle speeches (**Il. 4.234–420**), a model readily adopted in the exhortation poems of Tyrteus, the Spartan elegiac poet of the mid-seventh century BC.[126] Similar battle exhortations can be found in Herodotus, in which the "father of history" describes Themistocles and Harmokides encouraging their men to an honourable fight and to avoid the humiliation of a defeat.

It was Thucydides who introduced a "reinterpretation" of the function of the exhortation speeches in historiography, in that he did not care to reproduce the exact words spoken by the general. Rather, he looked to show first the character and intelligence of the general, followed by his own interpretation of the real reasons behind the outcome of the battle.[127] These rhetorical innovations transformed the Thucydidean exhortations into a model

121 https://bit.ly/2CflR2s [last accessed: 11.8.2020].
122 https://bit.ly/31ABWJU [last accessed: 11.8.2020].
123 https://bit.ly/3gL0l5O [last accessed: 11.8.2020].
124 https://bit.ly/2DXcxSn [last accessed: 11.8.2020].
125 Jon E. Lendon, "Battle Description in the Ancient Historians, Part II: Speeches, Results, and Sea Battles," *Greece and Rome* 64 (2017), 145–67 [here: 145–6]; Juan Carlos Iglesias Zoido, "The Battle Exhortation in Ancient Rhetoric," *Rhetorica: A Journal of the History of Rhetoric* 25 (2007), 141–58 [here: 142–4]; Nikolaos Mpezentakos, *Η Ρητορική της Ομηρικής Μάχης* [*The Rhetoric of Homeric Battle*] (Athens: Kardamitsa, 1996), part A, chapters 1–9; M. H. Hansen, "The Battle Exhortation in Ancient Historiography, Fact or Fiction?," *Historia* 42 (1993), 161–80 [here: 161–2].
126 Lendon (2017), 146; Iglesias Zoido (2007), 143. See also https://bit.ly/30P5Pa7 [last accessed: 12.8.2020].
127 Lendon (2017), 146–8; Iglesias Zoido (2007), 145–47; H. D. Westlake, *Individuals in Thucydides* (Cambridge: Cambridge University Press, 1968), 5–6.

in military oratory for subsequent generations, like Polybius and Sallust.[128] For others still, such as Quintus Curtius or Arrian, they served as a reason for displaying rhetorical skills, like in the pre-battle speeches that Alexander made before Issus and Gaugamela.[129] Thucydides is also known for his *lateral* battle exhortations at the Battle of Mantinea in 418 BC, where he puts the "Lacedaemonians encouraging one another both of themselves and also by the manner of their discipline in the war." A generation later, Xenophon recommended to members of the Greek Ten Thousand that they "Follow Heracles the Leader and summon one another on, calling each man by name. It will surely be sweet . . . to keep himself in remembrance among those whom he wishes to remember him."[130]

Caesar, that archetypal warrior-leader, almost without fail encourages his men before battle, regarding battle exhortation in fact a custom of war.[131] Also fascinating are Tacitus' dramatic speeches attributed to Germanicus and Arminius before the Battle of Idistavisto, during the Third Campaign against the Germanic tribe of the Cherusci in AD 16, and to Calgacus before the Battle of Mons Graupius in northern Scotland in AD 83 or 84.[132] Finally, a typical example of how military speeches evolved into a model for writing a *suasōria*, a deliberative speech advising a course of action in a historical situation, are the three extant *suasōriae* on battle-exhortation themes composed by Lesbonax of Mytilene, a Greek sophist and rhetorician in the time of Augustus.[133] For the Late Antique period, we should mention Publius

128 E. Keitel, "The Influence of Thucydides 7.61–71 on Sallust Cat. 20–21," *Classical Journal* 82 (1987), 293–300; C. W. Fornara, *The Nature of History in Ancient Greece and Rome* (Berkeley: University of California Press, 1983), chapter 4 ["The Speech in Greek and Roman Historiography"], 142–5.

129 Juan Carlos Iglesias Zoido, "The Pre-Battle Speeches of Alexander at Issus and Gaugamela," *Greek, Roman, and Byzantine Studies* 50 (2010), 215–41; N. G. L. Hammond, *Three Historians of Alexander the Great: The So-Called Vulgate Authors, Diodorus, Justin and Curtius* (Cambridge: Cambridge University Press, 1983); N. G. L. Hammond, *Sources for Alexander the Great: An Analysis of Plutarch's Life of Alexander and Arrian's Anabasis* (Cambridge: Cambridge University Press, 1993).

130 Thucydides, *History of the Peloponnesian War* (London: J. M. Dent and New York: E. P. Dutton, 1910), 5:69; Xenophon, *Anabasis* (New York: Appleton and Company, 1883), 6.5.24. Keith Yellin, *Battle Exhortation: The Rhetoric of Combat Leadership* (Columbia, SC: University of South Carolina Press, 2008), 40.

131 Yellin (2008), 101–9; John G. Nordling, "Caesar's Pre-Battle Speech at Pharsalus (B.C. 3.85.4): *Ridiculum Acri Fortius . . . Secat Res*," *The Classical Journal* 101 (2005/2006), 183–9.

132 Frances Butt Slaughter, "Direct and Indirect Speeches in Tacitus' *Historiae*" (Unpublished MA thesis, University of Richmond, Richmond, 1974), 6–90; N. P. Miller, "Dramatic Speech in Tacitus," *The American Journal of Philology* 85 (1964), 279–96.

133 Iglesias Zoido (2007), 154–5.

Herennius Dexippus' exhortation speeches for his fellow Athenians during the invasion and capture of the city by the Heruli in 267[134] and Ammianus Marcellinus' speech attributed to Julian on the eve of the Battle of Argentoratum (Strasbourg) against the Alamanni in 357. According to O'Brien, the latter speech "plays a significant part in Ammianus' strategy of building Julian up for imperial office."[135]

In ancient Rome, the *adlocūtiō* was an address given by the emperor to his massed soldiers during a special ceremony, either in a military camp or close to the battlefield, or even in Rome if political circumstances required it.[136] The Latin noun *adlocūtiō* (feminine, third declension) is an alternative form of *allocūtiō*, which means an address, consolation, or comforting speech.[137] It usually followed an ancient Greek and Roman ritual of purification by sacrifice called *lustratio exercitus*.[138] Modern researchers emphasize the depiction of the *adlocūtiō* in the Roman arts of statuary and coinage that portray the different characteristics of this ceremonial act. In sculpture, the *adlocūtiō* is often portrayed either simply as a single, life-size contrapposto figure of the emperor-general with his arm outstretched as a symbol of power and authority or as a relief scene on a podium addressing the army, like those seen in the columns of Trajan and Aurelius.[139] Such scenes also frequently appear on imperial coinage, where in the case known as an *adlocūtiō cohortium* ("address to the cohorts") the soldiers are depicted in a compact formation standing in front of emperor Caligula,[140] or as in the simple *adlocūtiō* in which emperor Galba and his soldiers and officers

134 Fergus Millar, "P. Herennius Dexippus: The Greek World and the Third-Century Invasions," *The Journal of Roman Studies* 59 (1969), 12–29.
135 Peter O'Brien, "Ammianus Marcellinus, the Caesar Julian, and Rhetorical Failure," *Cahiers des études anciennes* 50 (2013), 139–60.
136 Karaple (2010), 146.
137 https://bit.ly/2XKRycI [last accessed: 10.8.2020].
138 https://bit.ly/31GGWww [last accessed: 10.8.2020]. There is a description of the *lustratio exercitus* in Livy's *History of Rome*, 40.6: https://bit.ly/3ae6fd6 [last accessed: 10.8.2020].
139 Anthony Corbeill, *Nature Embodied: Gesture in Ancient Rome* (Princeton, NJ: Princeton University Press, 2004), 20–4; Inez Scott Ryberg, *Panel Reliefs of Marcus Aurelius* (New York: Archaeological Institute of America, 1967). For – perhaps – the most famous sculpture of this kind, that of Augustus of *Prima Porta*, a full-length portrait statue of Augustus that stands 2.08 meters tall and weighs 1,000 kg (discovered on 20.4.1863), see: Richard Brilliant, *Gesture and Rank in Roman Art: The Use of Gestures to Denote Status in Roman Sculpture and Coinage* (New Haven, CT: Connecticut Academy, 1963), 62–78.
140 See the example of the coin struck by Gaius (Caligula). AD 37–41. Æ Sestertius (27.99 g, 6h). Struck AD 37–38: https://bit.ly/3gJ2RcJ [last accessed: 10.8.2020].

are depicted in a more amiable (or restless?) atmosphere.[141] In all of the aforementioned examples, the emperor is depicted facing his troops on top of what was called a *tribunal*, which means a raised wooden or stone semicircular or square platform, or the elevation in the camp, from which the general addressed the soldiers and/or administered justice.[142]

Sadly, there is no depiction of a Byzantine emperor exhorting his troops, although of great interest is the portrayal of Joshua (a leadership model for Byzantine emperors) in the *Vatopedi Octateuch* (thirteenth century), codex 602 and folio 337, clad in military outfit and exhorting his officers and troops while leading them across the River Jordan.[143] Nevertheless, there are nine military speeches directed to imperial troops in Theophylaktos Simokattes' *History* that focus mainly on the wars of the empire with the Avars and the Slavs in the Balkans and with Persia in the East in the second half of the sixth century, including important data on various Turkish leaders.[144] We also find rousing speeches made by Heraclius during his wars against the Persian Empire, thanks to George of Pisidia's *Expeditio Persica* and to verse summaries of the most notable campaign speeches, which he included in his revised edition of Heraclius' dispatches and which are quoted almost verbatim by Theophanes. What is most important in Heraclius' speeches is the relationship of emperor and army to God and his resulting φιλανθρωπία (=benevolence), with which Heraclius wished to counterpose the tyranny and violence of the Persians.[145] Therefore, there is little doubt that George of Pisidia's military exhortations aimed to strengthen Heraclius' political theology as a divine ruler and, eventually, as the saviour of the empire of God on earth.[146]

141 See the example of the coin struck by Galba. AD 68–69. Æ Sestertius (35mm, 25.47 g, 6h). Struck circa December AD 68: https://bit.ly/30Gqf52 [last accessed: 10.8.2020].

142 https://bit.ly/33JfLnp [last accessed: 10.8.2020].

143 Karaple (2010), 149 and 442. There are some interesting leadership scenes in the *Joshua Rolls* (Pal.gr.431.pt.B) (tenth century), folios VII^r, X^r and XIII^r: https://digi.vatlib.it/view/MSS_Pal.gr.431.pt.B [last accessed: 14.8.2020].

144 Anna Kotlowska and Łukasz Rozycki, "The Role and Place of Speeches in the Work of Theophylact Simocatta," *Vox Patrum* 36 (2016), 353–82; Joseph D. C. Frendo, "History and Panegyric in the Age of Heraclius: The Literary Background to the Composition of the 'Histories' of Theophylact Simocatta," *Dumbarton Oaks Papers* 42 (1988), 143–56.

145 James Howard-Johnston, "Heraclius' Persian Campaigns and the Revival of the East Roman Empire," *War in History* 6 (1999), 1–44; Mary Whitby, "Defender of the Cross: George of Pisidia on the Emperor Heraclius and His Deputies," in: Mary Whitby (ed.), *The Propaganda of Power: The Role of Panegyric in Late Antiquity* (Leiden: Brill, 1998), 247–73; Suzanne Spain Alexander, "Heraclius, Byzantine Imperial Ideology, and the David Plates," *Speculum* 52 (1977), 217–37.

146 Yannis Stouraitis, "State War Ethic and Popular Views on Warfare," in: Yannis Stouraitis (ed.), *A Companion to the Byzantine Culture of War, ca. 300–1204* (Leiden: Brill, 2018), 59–91 [here: 71–5].

Figure 1.2 Gaius (Caligula). Struck AD 40–41. Laureate head left/Gaius standing left, extending right hand in gesture of address; behind him a *sella castrensis* (campstool); in front of him stand five soldiers. RIC I 48 (Courtesy of *Classical Numismatic Group, LLC*, www.cngcoins.com)

Figure 1.3 Galba. Struck circa December AD 68. Laureate head right, globe at point
of neck/ADLOCVTIO/S C in two lines in exergue, Galba, bareheaded in
military dress, standing right on low platform on left, haranguing troops.
RIC I 463 (Courtesy of *Classical Numismatic Group*, *LLC*, www.cng
coins.com)

Better studied and appreciated, however, are Procopius' *Wars of Justinian*, in which the historian uses pre-battle exhortations to prepare his readers for subsequent action – a particularly effective narrative tool for combat descriptions.[147] Pre-battle exhortations in Procopius are more prominent and numerous in the *Vandal Wars* than in the *Persian Wars*, where both Belisarius and Gelimer appeal to their men's emotions, patriotism, and personal bravery. Moreover, in a typical Thucydidean fashion, the *Wars* provide a means of understanding and evaluating the respective generals' performances and assessing the real causes of a victory or defeat.

The "practicalities" of exhortation speeches: where, when, how

One of the main duties and responsibilities of an emperor or a general was to encourage his troops by what we identified in the last section as δημηγορίαι προτρεπτικαί. Whether the exhortation speeches that have survived were trustworthy reproductions of the actual speeches delivered to the troops is beyond the scope of this study,[148] although it is fair to say that what modern historians get to read is – in all probability – a reconstructed and literary elaborated version of a much shorter speech that would have actually been circulated on the battlefield or what the emperor wanted to publish as his political propaganda. Nonetheless, that does not negate the fact that some sort of speeches were indeed delivered to troops, although the practicalities of the whole process have come under scrutiny, with historians underlining the impracticality of a leader delivering a long speech to massed troops of more than a few thousands.[149] However, the commander did address the troops, either in camp,[150] perhaps following the

---

147 Conor Whately, *Battles and Generals: Combat, Culture, and Didacticism in Procopius' Wars* (Leiden: Brill, 2016), 77–84, 134–9; Anthony Kaldellis, *Procopius of Caesarea: Tyranny, History, and Philosophy at the End of Antiquity* (Philadelphia, PA: University of Pennsylvania Press, 2004), 29–34.

148 Mogens Herman Hansen, "The Little Grey Horse: Henry V's Speech at Agincourt and the Battle Exhortation in Ancient Historiography," *Histos* 2 (1998), 46–63; W. K. Pritchett, "The General's Exhortation in Greek Warfare," in: *Essays in Greek History* (Amsterdam: J.C. Gieben, 1994), 27–109; Mogens Herman Hansen, "The Battle Exhortation in Ancient Historiography. Fact or Fiction?," *Historia: Zeitschrift für Alte Geschichte* 42 (1993), 161–80.

149 Edward Anson, "The General's Pre-Battle Exhortation in Graeco-Roman Warfare," *Greece & Rome* 57 (2010), 304–18; Hansen (1998), 59–61; Hansen (1993), 179.

150 Haldon (1990), 122–4; John F. Haldon, "The *Praecepta Militaria* of the Emperor Nikephoros II Phokas," in: Eric McGeer (ed. and trans.), *Sowing the Dragon's Teeth: Byzantine Warfare in the Tenth Century* (Washington, DC: Dumbarton Oaks, 1995), VI. 3.

emperor's military council with his generals,[151] or after the end of the religious service and the blessing of the standards.[152] If the force was small enough (perhaps up to 2,000),[153] the commander might have delivered some encouraging words to those already arrayed for combat.[154] If the force was too large, then the commander had other options; we read in Leo VI's *Tactical Constitutions*:

> When you are not otherwise occupied, you shall assemble the army by *droungoi* and by *tourmai*,[155] but not all at once in one place. Appropriate speeches should be addressed to them, either by yourself or their individual officers (=ἀρχόντων). Recall their past victories and their earlier successes to encourage them. Promise rewards and benefactions from Our Majesty and recompense for their loyalty to the state. Remind them, furthermore, of the commands given them and the other orders that they have received from you personally and from their own officers in each unit.[156]

Therefore, if the voice of the emperor/general were impossible to be heard by everyone in the army, then the order/speech would have been transmitted in writing[157] down the chain of command to the respective officers, a practice that has remained the same to this day. In addition, the right person to

151 *Naumachiae Syrianou Magistrou*, in Demetroukas (2005), 9.15.

152 In Leo's *Tactical Constitutions*, the exhortation comes after the blessing of the standards and the religious services and is included in the Constitution 13 ["About the Day before Battle"]: *Taktika*, in Dennis (2010), XIII. 1–4. The same for the *Strategikon*, in Dennis (1984), VII. ["Before the Day of the Battle"], 4.

153 Both authors of this study have served as conscripted soldiers doing their national service, and were both addressed *en masse* by their battalion (around 500–600 men strong) and regiment (around 1,000–1,200 men strong) commanders, whom they were able to hear very well.

154 We read in Leo VI's Constitution 14 ["About the Day of Battle"] that the general should "ride jauntily and confidently along the battle line, encouraging all by your words": *Taktika*, in Dennis (2010), XIV. 2. See also Georgios Chatzelis and Jonathan Harris (trans.), *A Tenth-Century Byzantine Military Manual: The Sylloge Tacticorum* (Oxon and New York: Routledge, 2017), 44.5.

155 Each army corps (*thema*) consisted of three *tourmai* (around 1,000 men each), each under a *tourmarches*; each *tourma* was then divided into three *droungoi* (between 200–400 men each), under a *droungarios*.

156 *Taktika*, in Dennis (2010), XIII. 4. Similar description in George T. Dennis (trans.), *Maurice's Strategikon, Handbook of Byzantine Military Strategy* (Philadelphia, PA: University of Pennsylvania Press, 1984), VII. 4.

157 *Strategikon*, in Dennis (1984), III. 11.

deliver the rousing speech to the troops, both before and during the battle, was the herald/cantor:

> The function of the heralds (=καντατόρων), it seems to us, is a useful one, inasmuch as before the battle they address the troops to encourage them and get them to recall their previous victories. When their speech is finished, each tagma should be formed and drilled.[158]
> Be sure [general] to select one soldier, competent and educated, for the position referred to as cantor. Assign him to move about quickly in the midst of the fighting to encourage the troops in the unit and to arouse them to enthusiasm by hortatory words according to the model that we have prescribed for you.[159]

The skills of a commander as a public speaker

Being a good public orator with developed rhetorical skills did not guarantee loyalty by the battle-hardened troops, whom the emperor/general was – practically – demanding to risk their lives for God, for himself, and for the empire; addressing the senators was one thing, inspiring the men to die in battle was something very different! Therefore, many ancient authors and almost all of the ancient military treatises on warfare dedicate a section to the oratorical skills of the ideal commander.

Homer felt that the great leader had "to be both a speaker of words and a doer of deeds."[160] For Hesiod (*Theogony*, composed c. 730–700 BC), it was Kalliope, the Muse who presided over eloquence and epic poetry, who "accompanies revered kings. Whosoever among sky-nourished kings is honoured by these daughters of great Zeus [=the Muses] and is beheld by them when he is born, for such a man they pour sweet dew upon his tongue, and from his mouth flow sweet *words*."[161] Xenophon believed that "it is neither numbers nor strength which wins victories in war; but whichever of the two sides it be whose troops, by the blessing of the gods, advance to the attack with stouter hearts," although he also emphasized that speeches alone do not ensure victory in the field.[162]

---

158 *Strategikon*, in Dennis (1984), II. 19.
159 *Taktika*, in Dennis (2010), XII. 98.
160 *Iliad*, IX. 443.
161 R. C. Hesiod, *Theogony* (Indianapolis: Hackett, 2015), 80–4.
162 Xenophon (1883), III. i. 42–3. Several examples on the importance of the exhortation speeches in: Xenophon, *Cyropaedia* (Pittsburgh: Patterson & Hopkins, 1810), II. i. 13; III. iii. 41; III. iii. 43; III. iii. 48–51; Yellin (2008), 7–10.

In the *Στρατηγικός* (General) of Onasander (writing ca. AD 60), a general should be "a ready speaker; for . . . if a general is drawing up his men before battle, the encouragement of his words makes them despise the danger and covet the honour."[163] Sextus Julius Frontinus (wrote the *Strategemata*, 1st c. AD) includes several examples of exhortation speeches that were delivered to troops in Antiquity and the advantageous effect these had on the morale of the troops.[164] According to the author of the early seventh-century *Strategikon*, "the general who possesses some skill in public speaking is able, as in the past, to rouse the weak-hearted to battle and restore courage to a defeated army."[165] In the *On Strategy*, Syrianos stresses that the general "should be manly in his attitudes, naturally suited for command, profound in his thinking, sound in his judgement, in good physical condition, hardworking, emotionally stable. He should instil fear in the disobedient, while he should be gracious and kind to the others."[166] For Emperor Leo VI, a general:

> should be capable of speaking and exhorting in public. I think that this ability is of the greatest benefit to the army. If the general, when he is drawing up his troops for battle, should encourage them by his words, he will often induce them to despise the terrors, even death itself. At the same time, he makes them eager to obtain the good and pleasant rewards.[167]

The anonymous author of the ca. 960 treatise *On Skirmishing* repeats that a perfect general should be able to address his men in "honeyed words."[168] Finally, around the end of the 1070s, Kekaumenos admonishes the young commander to be an assiduous reader of ancient works, so that he becomes known not only for his *ἀνδρείαν* (=bravery) and *εὐβουλίᾳ* (=good counsel, prudence) but also for his *γνῶσιν* (=means of knowing) and his *εὐγλωττία* (=fluency of speech).[169]

163　Onasander, *General*, I. 13: https://www.loebclassics.com/view/onasander-general/1928/pb_LCL156.341.xml.
164　S. Frontinus, *Strategemata*, I. i. 10; I. v. 15; I. xii. 3; III. i. 1; IV. v. 10; IV. vii. 30: https://books.google.co.in/books/about/The_Strategemata.html?id=XGDTzQEACAAJ&source=kp_book_description&redir_esc=y.
165　*Strategikon*, in Dennis (1984), VIII. 2.74.
166　*On Strategy*, in Dennis (1985/2008), 4.
167　*Taktika*, in Dennis (2010), II. 12; XX. 217. See also the Epilogue, 21 and 23. Very similar phrasing to Leo's can be read in the *Sylloge Taktikorum* (written ca. AD 930): Chatzelis and Harris (2017), 1.30.
168　*On Skirmishing*, in Dennis (1985/2008), chapter 23.
169　Kekaumenos, *Strategikon*, Dimitrios Tsougkarakes (trans.) (Athens: Agrostis and Kanake, 1993), 82–3.

Rhetorical topoi in building morale

To compare and contrast the content of the *Rhetorica Militaris* with the rest of the military treatises concerning their reference on battle exhortations, I will focus on the motive appeals or *rhetorical topoi* used. What sorts of things do the speakers emphasize or repeat to build morale among their troops? First, the speaker directly addressed his audience in a manner that resembles beseeching rather than ordering them, hence the meaning of the Latin term for our herald in Leo's *Tactical Constitutions* (*cantor/cantator* = to use enchantments, charms, incantations, to enchant, to charm). In the RM, the speaker calls his audience ἄνδρες (=men; 22.2, 55.2, 58), apparently to denote their maturity to go to war as opposed to the παιδιά (=young children), while the repeated use of the nouns συστρατιῶται (=fellow soldiers; 22.2, 22.5, 28.2, 28.4, 55.2), ἀδελφοί (=brothers; 22.2, 28.2, 37.1, 43.1, 52.1, 55.2) and τέκνα (=sons; 32, 36.3, 43.1) displays his desire to build a sort of a family atmosphere resembling that between father and son and to reinforce the image of the soldiers being the emperor's flesh and blood.[170] On top of that, the father and son metaphor suggests the desire of the commander to instil the same sort of τάξις (=discipline, order) that a father would teach his son.[171] The ἄνδρες Ῥωμαῖοι (=Roman men; 33, 49.3) is, undoubtedly, an honorific and charming address.

The address *commiilitones* (=fellow soldiers) has been traditionally attributed by Polyaenus to Caesar,[172] while Ammianus Marcellinus puts it in the mouth of the emperor Constantius II (reigned 337–61) when addressing his soldiers fighting the Alamanni over the Rhine in AD 354 and against the Quadi and Sarmatians across the Danube in AD 357.[173] Leo the Deacon has Nikephoros Phokas using the aforementioned term when exhorting his troops in Crete against the Arabs in AD 960, later against the Hamdanids of Aleppo, when Nikephoros assumed the imperial regalia following the death of Emperor Romanos II in AD 963 and on several other official occasions.[174]

---

170 On the Biblical origin of the father-son metaphors: Meredith L. D. Riedel, "Biblical Echoes in Two Byzantine Military Speeches," *Byzantine and Modern Greek Studies* 40 (2016), 207–22 [here: 216–7].

171 For the reforms in the Byzantine army of the tenth century, which included a vigorous attempt to instil the desirable τάξις, as attested in the military manuals of the period: Theotokis (2018), chapter 10.

172 Polyaenus, *Stratagems in War*, XXIII. 15, 16, 22: https://www.google.co.in/books/edition/ Polyænus_s_Stratagems_of_War/CntaAAAAYAAJ?hl=en&gbpv=1&dq=Polyaenus,+St ratagems+in+War&printsec=frontcover.

173 Ammianus Marcellinus, *History* (Cambridge, MA: Harvard University Press, 1950), XIV. 10.13; XVI. 12.9; XVI. 12.31.

174 Leo the Deacon, *History* (Washington, DC: Dumbarton Oaks, 2005), I. 6; II. 3; III. 5; IV. 11.

In Theodosius the Deacon's historical epic with encomiastic elements on the *Capture of Crete* (written in 963), we read about Nikephoros Phokas addressing his troops as *"Ῥώμης τὰ νεῦρα, τέκνα, σύνδουλοι, φίλοι"* (=Sinews of Rome, children, fellow slaves, friends).[175] Finally, in one of Constantine VII's military orations (ca. AD 950) to his soldiers and officers in the East, which was heavily influenced by the RM and Leo VI's *Constitutions*, the emperor reveals his ambition to accompany his soldiers on a future campaign, thus addressing them as "fellow cavalrymen, fellow infantrymen, and comrades in arms."[176]

A compelling way to raise the morale of the soldiers before battle is to remind them of previous victories, especially if they have defeated the enemy before. The aim is no other than to fill them with confidence and courage but also to remind them of their responsibility in emulating the achievements of their ancestors, especially when they have "big shoes to fill." We read in the RM:

> Our ancestors of old, those who once achieved many great successes, are still praised today for their skills in arms. May we do likewise, following in their footsteps, pursue glory, in order to reach it and be crowned with similar achievements. You see that, as I told you from the beginning, I am addressing you as your father, and to you, my true children, I wish your salvation. Therefore, you too hasten, along with your father, to call upon the heavenly powers, to show in battle the same strength, intention, courage and bravery, to do the same feats that transformed the Romans from a small nation to a great one, as they attacked the land of enemies and made it their own. That is why they are still praised for these achievements. So we too must follow the path of their conquests, to become equally worthy of praise.[177]

Strangely, there is no use of the rhetorical *topos* of reminding the soldiers of previous victories before the RM.[178] Only about two generations later, when Constantine VII dispatched his exhortations to his soldiers in the East, which were influenced – as we already mentioned – by the RM, do we see the emperor repeatedly reminding his soldiers of their (not of their ancestors')

---

175 Denis Sullivan (ed. and trans.), *The Rise and Fall of Nikephoros II Phokas, Five Contemporary Texts in Annotated Translations* (Leiden: Brill, 2019), 158–9.

176 Eric McGeer, "Two Military Orations of Constantine VII," in: John W. Nesbitt (ed.), *Byzantine Authors: Texts and Translations Dedicated to the Memory of Nicolas Oikonomides* (Leiden: Brill, 2003), 127, 130.

177 RM, 32. See also 6.1 and 49.5.

178 Karaple (2010), 252.

past victories over the Hamdanids of Aleppo. We read, for example,[179] "As I receive word of the surpassing renown of your exploits, men" and "What great things I have heard about you, and what great tidings have been brought back to me" or "you have set up such trophies as these against the enemy, you have striven for such victories as these, which have reached every corner of the world." Leo the Deacon also used this motif of past victories when Nikephoros Phokas was exhorting his troops outside the walls of the Cretan capital Chandax in 960, saying "Proof of my words [regarding the help of the Almighty] is our recent victory [after we landed on the island]."[180]

Reminding the soldiers of their past victories was coupled with the motive appeal of demeaning the enemies in the eyes of your troops in order, once again, to fill them with courage and hope that they would easily prevail in the upcoming battle. According to the RM:

> **25a.** The arguments coming from persons can be drawn from the religion, from the mode of life, and from the slander of the enemy army. . . . [**26.3**] Many of those who have deserted to us say that the enemy has gathered farmers and other craftsmen, hardly armed at all, to wage war against us.[181]

Syrianos repeats the aforementioned recommendation in his *Naumachica*, saying that the commander should "calumniate the enemy soldiers in a persuasive manner while praising his own troops."[182] Emperor Heraclius assured his troops of the destitute condition of the Persian army with these words: "Let us be aware, O brethren that the Persian army, as it wanders through difficult country is exhausting and debilitating its horses."[183] Moreover, the author of the treatise *On Skirmishing* has the commander addressing his men with the words "Let us show them [enemy] that they are attacking stronger men, that they are drawn up facing men who will strike rather than be struck."[184] Finally, in his propagandistic oration of 950, Constantine VII makes a similar point:

> How you [soldiers] were embroiled in combat not as if against men but as if triumphing over feeble women, succeeding not as in battle

179 McGeer (2003), 117.
180 Leo the Deacon (2005), I. 6.
181 RM, 26.3. See also 34, 44.5, 45.1.
182 Dain (1943), 9.15.
183 Cyril Mango and Roger Scott (trans.), *The Chronicle of Theophanes Confessor* (Oxford: Clarendon, 1997), 441.
184 *On Skirmishing*, in Dennis (1985/2008), chapter 23.

or in war, but rather dealing with men as though it were child's play, even though they were mounted on horses whose speed made them impossible to overtake, even though they were protected by equipment unmatched in strength and in craftsmanship.[185]

This image of the Arabs as effeminate warriors painted by Constantine, which served to promote himself and his reign in the eyes of not only his soldiers but the political establishment in Constantinople, is sharply contrasted by his writings in the *De Administrando Imperio*. The latter was a confidential and highly sensitive document commissioned by Emperor Constantine between 948–52 solely for the eyes of the heir to the throne, his son and future emperor Romanos. We read, "They [Fatimid Arabs of North Africa] are brave men and warriors, so that if they be found to the number of a thousand in an army, that army cannot be defeated (*αἥττητον*) or worsted (*ἀκαταμάχητον*)."[186]

Syrianos' recommendation to the commander to paint his enemies in the most derogatory way is contrasted by his suggestion to portray the Roman (he uses the Athenians versus the Persians as his example) soldier as the defender of the *patria* and the ultimate role model of a warrior. Hence, we read:

> So if the Persians, barbarians though they are, dared to do such things in search of temporary glory and honor, how can we not fight to the last man, not only for a temporary glory, but also for immortality, for the sake of our compatriots and ourselves? **10**. Because as much as we differ from them in terms of the knowledge of what is good, that much more we also demand the pains that a war brings.[187]

Most common are the commander's appeals to the martial, manly virtues: bravery, valour, and prowess. Closely connected with these motives is the public recognition that goes with them: honour, glory, and renown. According to Syrianos, glory and fame that come from martial prowess in the battlefield would accompany the men in this life and would be remembered by future generations:

> Just like the useful, likewise the glorious is divided according to what one does or does not do against the enemies. For example, if we fight,

---

185 McGeer (2003), 117.
186 *DAI*, in Moravcsik and Jenkins (1985), chapter 15.
187 RM, 45.9–10, 32–3.

then yes, we will uphold the glory we already have, but we will add even more. If some kind of ill repute accompanies us from the past, then we will get rid of it, while the chance of developing a bad reputation will not bear fruit either. On the contrary, if we do not fight, then whatever glory we already have will be fleeting, and the one we are seeking after will not come, the possible ill repute from the past will go on, while more will be added in the future. **3.** So the glorious should be elaborated according to the useful, not only from the positions that have already been formulated, but also from arguments and other.[188]

For the author of the *Strategikon*, "failure means swift death or flight, which is worse than death, whereas success brings gratification, material gain, fame, eternal memory."[189] Moreover, we read that a commander should "Make peace a time of training for war, and battle an exhibition of bravery," which is repeated in the *Tactical Constitutions* in that "When the time comes to take the field, you [general] will provide, not just a training exercise in manly valour, but an actual demonstration of it."[190] However, once again, Constantine VII's military orations offer the best example of the use of the aforementioned motifs in exhorting the troops: "You [soldiers] have set up such trophies as these against the enemy, you have striven for such victories as these, which have reached every corner of the world, and have made you famous not only in your native lands but in every city. Now your wondrous deeds are on every tongue, and every ear is roused to hear of them."[191]

In using the Byzantine army's Christian faith as a rallying cry, we emphasize another stark contrast between the soldiers of the empire and those of her enemies, that between Christians and "the Others." We observe the conflict between those who were righteous and those who were not, those who were faithful to the one true religion and those who were not and those who were "real" (or "ideal") soldiers and the "false" ones, a classic perspective of those engaged in defensive warfare.[192] We read:

> And I really wonder if someone, having seen how impious our enemies are, is not in a hurry to fight them with all his might. They have stripped off God or they are fighting against God. In any case, even if there are no others willing to fight against them, it is absolutely necessary for us

188 RM, 18.2–3. See also: 22.4, 36.4, 44.1–45.1.
189 *Strategikon*, in Dennis (1984), IV. 5.
190 *Strategikon*, in Dennis (1984), VIII. 2.64; *Taktika*, in Dennis (2010), XX. 129; also II. 16.
191 McGeer (2003), 117–18, 131.
192 Riedel (2016), 217–18.

to do so, who are characterized by piety and are always protectors of the law.[193]

We see very similar comments in Leo VI's treatise concerning the importance placed by the soldiers and the commanders in their belief in God over their polar opposite ["the Others"]:

> We indeed hold God as our friend who bears the power of balance in war. The foe are the very opposite because of their lack of faith in Him. If the heralds think of anything else along these lines, they should make use of it in their exhortations and admonitions. Such words uttered at the right time are very powerful in arousing spirits, more than a large amount of money.[194]

Moreover, we read in Constantine VII's 950 oration that it is the faith in the one true God that could only tip the balance of power decisively over to the Byzantine side, even if the empire's enemies were numerous and armed with "unmatched" armour:

> Even though they [Hamdanid Muslims of Aleppo] were protected by equipment unmatched in strength, equipment unmatched in craftsmanship, and lacked nothing at all of those things which bring security and cause astonishment. But since they were without the one paramount advantage, by which I mean hope in Christ, all of their advantages were reduced to nothing and were in vain.[195]

In the critical question in the back of the mind of every soldier in history: "For whom/what are we fighting?" (=ὑπέρ τίνος ο ἀγών), the Greek tragedian Aeschylus provided a short but definite answer to his fellow Greeks in his tragedy *Persians* (premiered in 472 BC), inspired as it was by the historic naval battle of Salamis eight years before: "On, you men of Hellas! Free your native land. Free your children, your wives, the temples of your fathers' gods, and the tombs of your ancestors. Now you are fighting for all you have."[196] Thirteen centuries later, Syrianos is also explicit about the motives that emboldened the Roman soldiers while facing enemies in

193 RM, 26.1.
194 *Taktika*, in Dennis (2010), XII. 57. See also *On Skirmishing*, in Dennis (1985/2008), chapter 15.
195 McGeer (2003), 117.
196 Aeschylus, *Persians* (New York: Start Publishing, 2013), 402–5.

battle: for their religion, for the Roman *genos* and their compatriots and co-religionists, for their emperor, for justice and for the expected reward. Now let us go through them one by one.

We read in the RM, "the barbarians who fight us do so because they are actually fighting our faith. Because if we believed in the same [God] as them, then they would not fight us."[197] The defensive character of the war against the empire's archenemy and the key role of religion in this issue is obvious here, and, moreover, Syrianos placed this paragraph under the chapter [9.2] on what is "just" (=δίκαιον). In most of the Byzantine treatises of military nature we have studied so far, we find explicit references on going to war for God and the faith and about the just cause of defending God and Orthodoxy from faithless (=ἄπιστα) nations such as the Muslims – the stark contrast between the Christians and "the Others" that we saw before. We read:

> The Romans . . . must be resolute in purpose and those <citizens> who have not actually gone off to war must campaign along with them against those people who blaspheme the emperor of all, Christ our God, and they must strengthen those waging war on His behalf against the nations by every means.[198]
> . . . it [is] unfair for the huntsmen to entice the hounds with the blood and the organs of the prey but to leave unrewarded the great spirit of those who suffer on behalf of our own people and for the unblemished faith of the Christians.[199]
> Therefore, have no fear, my men, have no fear, fill your souls with zeal and show the enemy who rely on the help of Beliar or Muhammad what those who put their faith in Christ can accomplish. Be the avengers and champions not only of Christians but also of Christ Himself, Whom they wickedly deny.[200]

However, it would be a mistake to consider this religious rhetoric in Byzantium the primary cause for the empire going to war or engaging in a defensive warfare against non-Christian enemies. According to Stouraitis, "it can plausibly be asserted that the prominent role ascribed to the defence of religion as the higher cultural value of the medieval Romans in the *Rhetorica militaris* remained fully subordinate to a perception of war as a political

197 RM, 10.1.
198 *Taktika*, in Dennis (2010), XVIII. 123. See also: XIV. 31; XVIII. 105.
199 *Sylloge Taktikorum*, in Chatzelis and Harris (2017), 50.3.
200 McGeer (2003), 118.

task."[201] In other words, the Roman concept of "just war" included preventive or retaliation measures against enemies on the Empire's vast frontiers in order to avoid potential attacks or to punish foreign peoples that raided imperial territory, regardless of whether they were Christian or non-Christian. Syrianos observes that the Byzantines should defend themselves in the name of justice against their enemies that not only ill-treated their faith but also continuously attacked their lands. We read in the paragraph immediately following the one about the defence of the faith:

> By performing these actions for the benefit of the fatherland, to which we owe so much, such as our progress and upbringing, but also to our parents, children and siblings, how could we honor it worthily, if we did not endanger our property, our toil, but also our own lives, which, after all, come from it?[202]

For the author of the RM, the Byzantines had the duty to preserve justice by imitating the virtue of their fathers in defending their *patria* and seeking to inflict the greatest punishment upon the enemies who wished to set their hands upon their lands.[203] In both the RM and the *On Strategy*, the loyalty is implied to the πατρίς, which takes more the meaning of a soldier's place of birth and locality. On the other hand, in the treatises of the *Strategikon*,[204] the *Tactical Constitutions of Leo VI*[205] and the *Sylloge Taktikorum*,[206] the soldiers were doing loyal service to the πολιτεία, which comes to be understood as the State.[207] The relationship between the sovereign and the soldiers is one of mutual love and respect, which the commander earned – no doubt – through his oratorical skills and his actions on the ground, as we saw earlier. On that point, let us repeat the following extract from Syrianos' *On Strategy*:

> [the general] should be manly in his attitudes, naturally suited for command, profound in his thinking, sound in his judgement, in good

201 I. Stouraitis, "Using the Bible to Justify Imperial Warfare in High-Medieval Byzantium," in: C. Rapp and A. Kulzer (eds.), *The Bible in Byzantium: Appropriation, Adaptation, Interpretation. Journal of Ancient Judaism Supplements*, vol. 25, no. 6 (Vienna: Vandenhoeck & Ruprecht, 2018b), 89–106. See also: I. Stouraitis, " 'Just War' and 'Holy War' in the Middle Ages. Rethinking Theory through the Byzantine Case-Study," *Jahrbuch der Österreichischen Byzantinistik* 62 (2013), 227–64; Stouraitis, "State War Ethic" (2018), 75–81.
202 RM, 11.1. See also: 37.8.
203 Syrianos leaves no doubt that the war for the *patria* is a 'just war': RM, 9.2; 11; 37.6; 38.
204 *Strategikon*, in Dennis (1984), VII. (A) 4.
205 *Taktika*, in Dennis (2010), XIII. 4.
206 *Sylloge Taktikorum*, in Chatzelis and Harris (2017), 36.2.
207 Karaple (2010), 306–7.

physical condition, hardworking, emotionally stable. He should instil fear in the disobedient, while he should be gracious and kind to the others.[208]

The same author is also explicit in the RM that the aforementioned love and respect between the commander and his troops should be reciprocal:

As I have loved and protected you, my good and valiant comrades-in-arms, in the same way that a father does, it is impossible for you to fully learn it from anyone else. Because you have to remember that while you were sleeping at night, I was awake, and when you were resting from your daily toils, I struggled even harder. What was I doing? I was looking out for your interests, now walking around the palisade, now inspecting the ditches, and the like respectively, taking care of your safety. Why [was I doing] all this? To prevent the enemies from attacking the army at night, after having escaped our attention. **3.** For these reasons, it is necessary for you, just as children do, to follow our commands and understand that these deeds are your salvation. For I am fully convinced that, if you listen to this speech with the same goodwill and go immediately and take action, everything will turn out well for you.[209]

This is reiterated in the *Sylloge Taktikorum*,[210] while Kekaumenos urges the general "not to be afraid of death, if it is to die for the homeland [πατρίδα] and the emperor – on the contrary, to be more afraid of the dishonouring[211] and reprehensible[212] lifestyle."[213] Emperor Constantine VII also writes in his (c. 958–59) treatise on *Imperial Military Expeditions* of similar calls for the soldiers to show their true devotion and love for God and their emperor, after the latter had been received with honour and pomp in base camp during a military expedition.[214] Moreover, Syrianos presents this loyalty and obedience to the sovereign as a critical aspect of the Byzantine soldier's character, compared to his enemies, who were motivated by fear instead. We read:

I am referring to when we entered the battle at dusk and worked every night as if it was daytime, when you showed obedience and absolute

208 *On Strategy*, in Dennis (1985/2008), ch. 4.
209 RM, 36.2–3.
210 *Sylloge Taktikorum*, in Chatzelis and Harris (2017), 36.2.
211 αἰσχρῶς: causing shame, dishonouring, reproachful.
212 ἐπιψόγως: exposed to blame, blameworthy.
213 *Strategikon*, in Tsougkarakes (1993), 72–3.
214 Haldon (1990), 124–5.

discipline to us, considering fatigue as normal. . . . And behold, here are our enemies. Although they seem to be ready to attack us, in reality they are probably afraid of us. **6.** And I assure you that I see them moving with great hesitation, as if motivated only by the fear of the whip.[215]

It is interesting to make the comparison with the *Strategikon*'s description of the "Scythians," whom the author depicts as a nation "governed not by love but by fear" and who "prefer to prevail over their enemies not so much by force as by deceit."[216] We can also read similar demeaning depictions of the Persians, who "obey their rulers out of fear, and the result is that they are steadfast in enduring hard work and warfare on behalf of their fatherland."[217]

Imperial soldiers also perceived it as their duty to fight for the defence of their compatriots, and Syrianos writes about ten times in his RM [ὁμόφυλοι: 9.2–3, 12; 20.3; 35.1; 37.7; 45.5; 45.9; 52.2; ἀδελφοὺς ἡμῶν: 36.8] about the love towards them within the spirit of the "just war" to defend them from aggression. We read in Syrianos' work:

> So if we too take part in the teachings of God with our faith, let us love our brothers and sisters, and let us give our lives for one another and our co-religionists, so that by our actions we may become true disciples of Christ. **9.** But even for those who do not understand the divine law exactly like that, because Christ prevented Peter from using his knife, we should resort to the use of weapons as a last recourse, for the common good and in exceptional circumstances. **10.** The laws are good, and above all the laws that come from God himself, and we all strive to obey them. Indeed, what could be more useful to people than the law of God? A law gave value to the Maccabees.[218]

The emphasis here is on the neighbourly love that should be as strong as the love between brothers, to a point that you are ready to sacrifice your life for your neighbour. Yet the reference to the Maccabees in this paragraph draws explicit parallels to the Deuteronomy 20 and the Old Testament notion of "Holy War" as ordained by God to eradicate the oppressors of the "chosen people." However, as Stouraitis has pointed out, in ninth-century

---

215 RM, 44.4–6.
216 *Strategikon*, in Dennis (1984), XI. 2.
217 *Strategikon*, in Dennis (1984), XI. 1.
218 RM, 36.8–10. Compare with *Taktika*, in Dennis (2010), II. 31; XII. 57; XIV. 31; XVIII. 19, 41, 127; XX. 72; *Sylloge Taktikorum*, in Chatzelis and Harris (2017), 44.6; 50.3; McGeer (2003), 132. See also Karaple (2010), 309–12.

Byzantium, God's word and its relationship to warfare were understood in very different terms, to the point where the New Testament reference to Jesus and Peter demonstrates the anti-violent motif that Syrianos wished to emphasize in his work.[219] The latter rejects any connection between the sacrifice of the soldier in defence of his compatriots and a notion of martyrdom or other spiritual reward, pointing rather to war as an act of love in correspondence to the New Testament ideal of neighbourly love rather than a prerequisite to achieving martyrdom.[220] The act of killing in warfare contradicted God's will and law and was considered as the work of the devil and a great sin.[221]

The predominant perception regarding God's role in war in Byzantium is that He aids the righteous who strive to protect or restore the territories of the divinely protected Byzantine Empire. In the RM, therefore, we see God repeatedly been depicted as the "ultimate" sovereign or leader of the imperial armies: "we march against them [enemies] with greater courage, being on the right path to victory, under the guidance of God. At this point, we will put an end to the words, as God and the general have taken over the management of things together."[222] God is also seen as the ultimate arbiter of victory: "When delivering a triumphal speech, we must begin by thanking God, to whom the present victory is due,"[223] who also redresses misconducts of the past: "Then, thirdly, we must tell the soldiers that even if God punished them for something bad they did in their lives, if they choose to be in God's way again, then He too will fight with them for redress."[224] The bottom line is that "we trust in Him, we are guided by Him, and with His help we will overcome our enemies."[225] There are numerous examples of portraying God and the Theotokos as ultimate leaders of the imperial armies in the early and middle Byzantine sources, but there is no need to list them all here.[226]

---

219 Stouraitis, "Using the Bible" (2018), 96–100.
220 No mention of martyr status is made in Leo VI's reference to: "The bodies of the soldiers who have been killed in battle are sacred, especially those who have been most valiant in the fight on behalf of Christians." *Taktika*, in Dennis (2010), XX. 72. Those soldiers who died in battle were pronounced blessed (=μακάριοι) "because they have not preferred their own lives over their faith and their brothers." *Taktika*, in Dennis (2010), XIV. 31.
221 *Taktika*, in Dennis (2010), prologue. See also: I. Stouraitis, *Krieg und Frieden in der politischen und ideologischen Wahrnehmung in Byzanz (7–11. Jahrhundert)*. Byzantinische Geschichtsschreiber, 5 (Vienna: Fassbaender, 2009), 191–3.
222 RM, 44.7.
223 RM, 55.1–2.
224 RM, 56.2.
225 RM, 50.3.
226 Karaple (2010), 271–7.

The Old Testament (see Deuteronomy 20) view of God as a leader of the armies on the battlefield and the ultimate judge, which was merged with the New Testament notion of "just war" and self-defence, is how Syrianos interpreted divine intervention in the act of war. Only if the war was just, meaning that they strove to "right the wrongs" against them, and the soldiers and officers were righteous was God going to lead the imperial armies to victory; otherwise, He would lead them to their demise. Leo's *Tactical Constitutions* provides us with an analytical insight into the Byzantine notion of "just war":[227]

> **30.** We must always embrace peace for our own subjects, as well as for the barbarians, because of Christ, the emperor and God of all. If the nations also share these sentiments, stay within their own boundaries, and promise that they will not take unjust action against us, then you too refrain from taking up arms against them. Do not stain the ground with the blood of your own people or that of the barbarians. . . . We must always, if it is possible on our part, be at peace with all men, especially with those nations who desire to live in peace and who do nothing unjust to our subjects.

This is immediately followed by:

> **31.** But if our adversary should act unwisely, initiate unjust hostilities, and invade our territory, then you do indeed have a just cause, inasmuch as an unjust war has been begun by the enemy. . . . It is they who have provided the cause by unjustly raising their hands against those subject to us. Take courage then. You will have the God of justice on your side."

For Syrianos, the punishment of the evildoers is one of the just reasons to go to war, as it immediately follows the zeal for the faith and the sacrifice for the fatherland and the emperor that we mentioned previously. The author is explicit that

> It is terrible to tolerate the injustices of your enemies without defending yourself, but at the same time to seek revenge for the insults you have suffered. Because the more we tolerate their insults, the more we attract them to continue to come against us.[228]

---

227 *Taktika*, in Dennis (2010), II. 29–31.
228 RM, 13.

He insists that all injustices of the past must be avenged and any future be prevented[229] – the idea of revenge is at the core of Syrianos' arguments "For whom/what are we fighting?" (=*ὑπέρ τίνος ο ἀγών*). Moreover, he considers freedom a value that should be protected and cherished by the people of God, to be contrasted by the deprivation of one's freedom and property, which he considers a *μέγα κακόν* (=great evil).[230] Finally, Syrianos calls on the soldiers to live up to the reputation of their fathers and preserve justice, as "many times against the same enemies, they [ancestors] did not remain indifferent to what was happening, but they campaigned and punished them in an even harsher way."[231]

On the topic of "just war," Onasander emphasizes that

> the causes of war, I believe, should be marshalled with the greatest care; it should be evident to all that one fights on the side of justice. For then the gods also, kindly disposed, become comrades in arms to the soldiers, and men are more eager to take their stand against the foe.[232]

The author of the *Strategikon* is also unambiguous that "The cause of war must be just"[233] (=*δικαίαν δεῖ την ἀρχήν του πολέμου γίνεσθαι*), while for the author of the *Sylloge Taktikorum*, the general

> [must] truly be peaceful and sympathetic, because, at the beginning of the war, the generals should always be careful that they may become illustrious by fighting for the right cause, and not for the hope of earnings or profit. For it is then that men face hardships more willingly, and God becomes favourable and a comrade of the army.[234]

Finally, the feeling of justice is eminent in the *Strategikon* of Kekaumenos, who writes "Those under your control must learn to be prudent, and imitate your life – because the weapons of war is justice."[235]

As fear of killing and being killed in battle would have terrified any soldier from the dawn of humankind to the modern period, his primeval anxiety about the salvation of his soul would have had to be tamed somehow to maintain order and discipline within the ranks. Although Leo VI does not

---

229 RM, 28.2–3.
230 RM, 39.
231 RM, 37.8.
232 Onasander, ch. IV.
233 *Strategikon*, in Dennis (1984), VIII. B' 12.
234 *Sylloge Taktikorum*, in Chatzelis and Harris (2017), 1.27.
235 *Strategikon*, in Tsougkarakes (1993), 88–9.

use the term *jihad* or *holy war* anywhere in his *Tactical Constitutions*, he is aware that his Muslim foes are offered spiritual rewards, a recompense given by God for the moral quality of their efforts if they die in battle, which he identifies as compensation (*μισθός*: to mean a spiritual rather than a monetary pay). He contrasts these characteristics of Islamic military recruitment favourably with the Byzantine situation, wishing, no doubt, for his compatriots to emulate the voluntary nature and enthusiasm for war against infidels.[236] Yet it would be far from the truth to claim that Leo wished the Church to acclaim for the imperial soldiers the status of martyrs.

Throughout treatises of military nature like Leo VI's *Tactical Constitutions*, the *Anonymous Treatise on Skirmishing* and the Imperial harangues attributed to Emperor Constantine VII, those who die in battle were considered perpetually blessed (=*μακάριοι*) "because they have not preferred their own lives over their faith and their brothers."[237] We read in the RM:

> To the soldiers, then, if the general is giving a speech to them: "I am also grateful for your virtues, the zeal you showed, the passion, the bravery, the perseverance, the fact that you fought as befits heroes and, seeing this, God rewarded you with victory."[238]

Yet, as Byzantine authors eagerly condemned the (Old Testament) idea of God as a warmonger who ordained war against other people, Christians or non-Christians, they equally denounced the notion that war could become a means to remission of sins and hence martyrdom.

As Stouraitis has pointed out, in the handful of recorded cases of battle exhortations that we find in the Byzantine sources in which the spiritual reward from God was highlighted, in none of these do we find the principle that God had ordained the waging of the war against the enemy because of his religion.[239] What we do see, however, is for divine recompense to be dependent on the soldier's peaceful nature and piety rather than the killing of an infidel, as war and the act of murder of any human were considered sinful and the contrivances of the devil.[240] Therefore, as Christian soldiers dreaded death and the killing in battle, they also regarded the idea of divine recompense as a means of "psychological support" that could "offset" the sinful act of killing in defence of the divinely protected empire. This idea

236 *Taktika*, in Dennis (2010), XVIII. 122–3.
237 *Taktika*, in Dennis (2010), XIV. 31; McGeer (2003), 132.
238 RM, 55.4. See also: 8.3.
239 Stouraitis (2013), 243–6.
240 *Taktika*, in Dennis (2010), prologue.

served similar purposes with the religious acts of fasting and praying before battle,[241] which – needless to say – were employed against Christian and non-Christian enemies alike. For that reason, therefore, Leo instructed the Byzantine generals to "accustom" (=εθίζεστε) their soldiers to the correct faith, as this will expedite them to "easily overcome the distress of thirst and the lack of food, and of excess cold or heat . . . and for their pains they will store up compensations (μισθόν) from God himself and from His kingdom."[242]

Leo VI is also fully aware of the desire of the Muslims to obtain material goods: "Because of the booty they have reason to expect, and because they do not fear the perils of war, this nation is easily gathered together in large numbers from inner Syria and all of Palestine."[243] The collection of booty had always been a significant incentive for campaiging armies, and it is clear that every author places an importance on its control. As Haldon notes, the attraction of collecting booty frequently appears as an inducement to Byzantine troops, although it is never mentioned as a motive for recruitment, as in the case of the Arabs.[244] Syrianos puts the following pertinent argument in the mouth of the general when exhorting his troops to battle:

> If we defeat the enemies, not only will we preserve the goods that belong to us, but also at the same time we will acquire what belongs to the enemies. On the other hand, if we renounce the war, we may temporarily save our lives by choosing to flee, but soon all together and our families will be destroyed.[245]

This should be coupled with the author's explanation of what is "useful" in exhorting the men to war apart from the public speeches: "

> Beneficial for the war are not only these made up speeches, but also others, such as forcing some of the enemy's deserters to tell our own during the siege that the besiegers or the besieged lack the necessary

---

241 Karaple (2010), 67–89.
242 *Taktika*, in Dennis (2010), XVIII. 19. There are interesting similarities with the late seventeenth-century Ottoman treatise "Advice to Commanders and Soldiers," which forms part of a much larger work entitled *Mi'yârü'd-Düvel ve Misbârü'l-Milel* ["Standards of States and Probe of Nations"], written by a junior military officer in the Ottoman armourer corps, Esirî Hasan Ağa (1653/54–1720s): "A real soldier endures hot and cold, rain and mud, hunger and thirst and never gives up and does his best to perform his tasks. . . . Innumerable rewards to those who die [in battle against infidels] in the afterlife" Yildiz and Theotokis (2018), 133.
243 *Taktika*, in Dennis (2010), XVIII. 126.
244 Haldon (2014), 374.
245 RM, 28.4.

food, or that there is gold in the city, and silver and other precious goods, which the soldiers long for.[246]

For the author of the *Strategikon*, the general should also make "suitable speeches . . . promising rewards from the emperor, and recompense for their loyal service to the state,"[247] while in the *Sylloge Taktikorum*, we read that the general "[must] encourage and rouse the men for battle, announcing to them the rewards and honours given by the emperor and the wage on behalf of the nation."[248] In a similar fashion, Leo VI emphasizes that the general should "Promise rewards and benefactions from Our Majesty and recompense for their loyalty to the state."[249] One exception is, perhaps, the *Military Precepts* of Nikephoros Phokas, where the author gives precise instructions on how to tackle such a notorious habit among the troops, no doubt being fully aware that it goes against the battlefield discipline (=τάξις) that the Byzantine military establishment of the mid-tenth century was eager to instil in its troops;[250] for Phokas, looting and war booty were necessary evils.

Finally, we understand that the rewards from the emperor were not only material but also moral (offices, honours etc.), in what Syrianos advises the general to highlight to his soldiers in his exhortation speech:

> To the soldiers, then, if the general is giving a speech to them: "I am also grateful for your virtues, the zeal you showed, the passion, the bravery, the perseverance, the fact that you fought as befits heroes and, seeing this, God rewarded you with victory." **5.** It is appropriate, after all these thanks, first to praise them all together, and then those who displayed excellence on the battlefield by name, then once again return to the common praise for the whole army, and finally make the present victory look like the foundation stone for future military successes.[251]

In all of the treatises that we have examined so far, the following point is made abundantly clear: those who are brave; righteous and willing to fight and die for God, the emperor and the *patria* will receive ample recompense. On the other hand, those who are unwilling to do what is expected of them will be branded as cowards and will receive contempt from their compatriots and wrath and punishment from God and the emperor.

246 RM, 23.
247 *Strategikon*, in Dennis (1984), VII. 4.
248 *Sylloge Taktikorum*, in Chatzelis and Harris (2017), 44.5.
249 *Taktika*, in Dennis (2010), XIII. 4.
250 *Praecepta Militaria*, in McGeer (1995), II. 7–8.
251 RM, 55.4–5. See also: 17; 36.4; 45.

Note on the translation

There are now few sources in Byzantine history that have not been translated into English, which is also the *lingua franca* of our time. The study in question was based on one of them, which bears the conventional title "Encouraging public speeches," a ninth-century work which is attributed to Syrianos magistros.

For our translation, we used both critical versions of the work that have been written to date, including the old version of Köchly but also the modern one of Eramo. Eramo's edition also offers an Italian translation of the text. We tried to stay close to the meaning of what is in general an overly sophisticated Byzantine text in order to give a comprehensible translation to the reader but also pleasant to a degree, which would be a guide to how a Byzantine general motivated his troops before a critical battle or military campaign.

The structure of the translation follows the corresponding version of Eramo rather than Köchly's, since the original text has been further edited using codices that Köchly did not have available. After all, Köchly relied on just two codices for the *Rhetorica Militaris* version, *Parisinus 2522* and *Bernensis 97*, while Eramo also used the very important *Laurentianus LV.4* and a number of others. It is clear that the structure of Eramo's text is probably the best we have available, which is why we have kept the paragraph breaks in line with her Italian translation.

Apart from Eramo's Italian translation, this work has never been translated into any modern language before, except for some excerpts – Chapters I–III into German shortly after the middle of the nineteenth century by Köchly and Rüstow.

The language of the original text is extremely rich, and every effort has been made to convey the complex meanings and literary structures to the reader with precision and sharpness. Where it was deemed intentional, there are linguistic comments in the form of footnotes to help the reader get a clearer meaning of a sentence in the text.

The purpose of our translation is to make the text of Syrianos magistros accessible to any scholar who does not have the reading skills necessary to go through the original text in the medieval Greek language, so that it can be studied together with other works of the same genre and, hopefully, shed more light on an aspect of war and political propaganda in this critical period for the history of the Byzantine Empire. The means by which the Byzantine military leaders used to exhort their troops before a decisive conflict or the beginning of a campaign included elements that have nothing to envy of ancient Greek rhetoric, and we hope to have rendered them satisfactorily in English.

Hortatory public speeches
Drawing their arguments from various sources

1.1 What I have set as my goal to explain regarding the practical part of the whole science of governance, has been said. As for the rhetorical (Logical) part, it is divided into the unwritten and the written. By "unwritten" I define what is expressed directly, in person, with the voice,[1] while, on the other hand, "written" is expressed through the written word. **2.** Each of these two is again divided into two further parts, the one about speaking in the public assembly and the epistolic one – because sometimes a public speech may be delivered in writing, either due to embarrassment or weakness[2] or inexperience or some other impediment of the speaker. Public speaking is when the speech is addressed to a specific city or an assembled army, while with the epistolic (genre) we address one or two persons, or generally a small number of individuals. Sometimes, though, we may also use the epistolic genre to address a large number of people, as for example when Paul wrote to the Hebrews. **3.** Some of the public speeches are "civil,"[3] while others are "military." I define as civil those that make citizens better, either by encouraging them to(wards) virtue or by preventing them from evil, and about which we will talk later, while I define as military those that make soldiers more willing to go to war, and about which I'm going to talk [now]. **4.** The same style of public speech as that with which a general addresses his soldiers for war may also be used by the political leader[4] addressing the citizens, whenever he urges them to fight when the enemy is at the gates. In a similar manner, a general can resort to political speeches, when the soldiers do not comply[5] with the laws and customs of the city.

---

1 Alternatively: speech.
2 ἀσθένεια: want of strength, weakness or feebleness.
3 πολιτικοί: befitting a citizen, civic, civil, statesmanlike.
4 ἄρχων: ruler, commander; as official title: chief magistrate.
5 πολιτεύονται, from πολιτεύομαι: to act as a citizen, take part in the government.

2.1 Every public speech, whether written or oral, political or military, must be clear and free from any ambiguity, so that none of the listeners can misunderstand the meaning. **2.** Regarding the epistles, those addressed to subordinates should be as clear as the public speeches, and those addressed to rulers of states, even if the recipient has oratorical skills,[6] these should also be clear, unless you consider that some ambiguity[7] or equivocal[8] expression is appropriate for that particular circumstance, so that later you can claim that you did not write exactly this thing, as it was expressed with that specific word, but with the given ambiguity you meant something different. **3.** For example, the enemies wrote that they would attack[9] the city if the citizens do not hand over its treasures to them. The citizens made that promise. However, when the time to do battle had passed and the former demanded that the citizens give them the treasures, the latter replied that they would certainly give them those that were on the statue of the city. Examples must also be drawn from history. **4.** There is a foreign nation called the Phoenicians, who it is said also founded Carthage. When they sailed to Libya at some point, they asked the locals to admit them [into the city] "day and night." And the locals accepted this. When this time of "one day and a night" passed, the locals said they had to leave, and the Phoenicians claimed that it was not what they (the locals) really had agreed on, but they could stay there forever, as the former took this literary to mean "day and night," while the latter interpreted it as "forever." For the phrasing can support either meaning.

3.1. Therefore, as far as public epistles are concerned, and those which are addressed to the rulers of foreign nations, what we have written so far should suffice, as we do not intend to write more on the subject of epistles. So let us from now on talk about public speeches, which undoubtedly concern pragmatism. **2.** I do not ignore that Hermogenes, and other rhetoricians before and after him, argue that pragmatism is a situation in which you can talk about future issues, but at the same time to compose the appropriate counter-arguments from the exact same premises. **3.** We, however, who write about war according to pragmatism, will not construct opposite[10] arguments (and how could we?), but will deal only with exhortations to war, which is one of the two parts of the war-peace question.[11] For that

---

6 ἐσπουδακέναι, from σπουδάζω: to study, to be well-versed, eager.

7 ἀμφιβολία: ambiguity.

8 ὁμωνυμία: an equivocal word.

9 ἐπιθέσθαι, from ἐπιτίθημι: make an attack.

10 τἀναντία, from ἐναντίος: opposite.

11 πρόβλημα: a conundrum, a practical or theoretical problem; in the *Logic* of Aristotle, a question as to whether a statement is so.

reason, we have disregarded[12] any mention of the refutation [of war]. **4.** If one wanted to talk about peace as well, one could construct his reasoning with the same arguments, as we did with the ones about war, from the point of view of the lawful and the just *et cetera*. That is all.

4.1. Just like the farmers, who, when they are going to sow, first work the land, so that it is in a suitable condition to receive the seeds, likewise those who prepare an elaborate speech take care to find the right words and figures of speech, to make the listeners more susceptible to accepting their arguments thereafter. Of these initial parts of speech, one is called the prelude (=*προοίμιον*), the other preliminary exposition (=*προδιήγησις*), and the third the preface (=*προκατασκευή*). **2.** The prelude is the part of speech that serves to lay the foundations. The preamble (=*προκατάστασις*), or the preliminary exposition, is a part of speech that is placed after the preface, through which we lay down what has preceded the event, what is useful both in the preface and in the presentation of the case (=*προβολή*). The preface is essentially an outline of the points that will be elaborated later. The other part of the preface is not necessary for what we are interested in here.

5.1. The most powerful among those preludes concerning prestige,[13] and the ones that should be used more frequently, are first of all, those that show the paternal disposition of the general towards his army, that he, leaving aside his personal interest, always acts for the common good, enquiring, investigating, working hard, being vigilant, thinking what not to say and what not to do, as all these actions ensure that soldiers will be more disciplined. Secondly, those that are used to show the positive attitude of the army towards the general. Thirdly, the ones that blame those who bear the mistakes of others, but do not punish those who are responsible for them. **2.** Among the preambles, those that confirm the prelude and advance the continuity of the discourse are also useful. In fact, they are a reminder of the positive disposition of the general towards the army, reminiscent of his achievements, such as his diligence and vigilance: the army's efforts and achievements are due to the soldiers' obedience to him, while they reinforce the aversion towards those who defer[14] from going to war, and affirm the injustices committed by the enemies.

6.1. With regard to the prelude, the preamble and the preface, what we have already written is enough. Because not all parts of the preface are useful, like the other parts, to say more about them. In fact, since the situation is an urgent one, not only is this or that part of the prelude omitted, but

---

12 *παρήκαμεν*, from *παρίημι*: pass unnoticed, disregard.
13 *ὑπόληψις*: good or bad reputation, public opinion.
14 *ἀναβαλλομένων*, from *ἀναβάλλω*: put off, delay a thing in which oneself is concerned.

in some instances it is omitted in its entirety. Indeed, many times we begin with the preamble, as follows: "How many and what kind of military operations you have undertaken during this war, everyone already knows that very well. Therefore, if you have the same will now, remembering your previous achievements, let you make new, similar [achievements]. That is why I speak to you, urging you to fight." **2.** Sometimes, when the preamble is missing, we begin the discourse from the preface, for example: "What I am going to tell you is this: now that the enemy has been arranged [in battle] to fight us, it is absolutely necessary to stand with greater vigour against them, and to display with our actions the courage of our soul." **3.** And not only can we begin from this point, but also from the narrative,[15] for example: "Our enemies have already appeared, looking for war. That is why we must fight them as bravely as we can, and show them that we are unconquered[16] in the war." And what we have said for these things is enough.

7.1. In general, a speech that follows the principles of pragmatism consists of the following six elements: question, proposition,[17] position,[18] argument,[19] development[20] and syllogism.[21] **2.** The question we want to talk about, for example, is war. In this case the proposition is the exhortation to war, that is, why it is necessary to fight. The position is how the above proposition is elaborated, for example: "it is fair to defend ourselves against those who wrong us." The argument is the explanation that further supports the position, for example: "justice is good and suited only to men." Development is the way that the argument is advanced, for example: "There are many who, even after death, are praised and honoured for their justice, such as Aristides and whoever else is celebrated by the Greeks for the same reasons." The syllogism is the part where development is elaborated, for example: "If the Greeks were defending justice, how can we not do the same with all our might? In fact, we can brag[22] about it much more than anyone else!"

8.1. Since the question and the proposition are relatively simple, the explanations we gave above were just as simple. So we will talk about the other parts of the speech, how each of them is used, but also about the differences between them. We will do this not only with a didactic exposition,[23] but also in a practical way, through examples, both for the sake of clarity,

---

15 *διήγησις*: narration, narrative.
16 *ἀήττητον*, from *ἀήσσητος*: unconquered, not beaten.
17 *προβολή*: putting forward of a plea or case.
18 *κεφάλαιον*: chief or main point, the topic of argument.
19 *ἐπιχείρημα*: argument, dialectical proof.
20 *ἐργασία*: working at, making, developing.
21 *ἐνθύμημα*: contemplation, rhetorical syllogism drawn from probable premises.
22 *καλλωπιζόμεθα*, from *καλλωπίζω*: (metaph.) pride oneself in or on a thing.
23 *διδασκαλικῶς*: in a didactic manner.

but also to show the abundance of similar [examples/elements]. Because the motives of a speech actually offer a wealth of arguments to the one who intends to speak in this way. **2.** There are six main points: the lawful, the just, the useful, the possible, the glorious, and the future outcome.[24] **33.** Lawful means to resort to an existing law that is appropriate to the issue under consideration, for example: "There is a law that subjects the deserter to the capital punishment." Just means to resort to the law of nature, appropriate to the issue under consideration, for example: "It is just to take care of one's parents or to defend the homeland." By useful is meant that which is somehow beneficial to us. Possible is what can happen. Glorious is what can bring glory, for example valour. Many times interest and glory can take each other's place and meaning. As for the future outcome, it is when we formulate an argument based on either of the possible outcomes of a conflict, for example: "If we engage in a battle, whether we emerge as the losers or the winners, this conflict is beneficial to us. Because we can hope for a greater reward after death than what goods we have in this life."

9.1. What is included in each of the points has already been said. It will now be explained in how many ways each of them can be divided, with the exception of the future outcome. The lawful is divided into two parts, the written one usually called law, and the unwritten one usually known as ethos (custom). The written law prevails over the unwritten; for the written one is drafted by the wise, while the latter is composed by any random man, and the former [is drafted based on] logic, while the latter is put together by time. **2.** The just stems from the zeal of faith, from the love for the homeland, the love for the fellow compatriots,[25] from the need to punish the unjust (enemies). Each of them is the just. **3.** From zeal for the faith come the goods of God, the love for the homeland is associated with worldly goods, for example birth, upbringing (education) and the like, love for your compatriots out of a disposition for goodness, and its retribution through deeds, when the time comes, while the punishment of the wrongdoers comes from their own acts of evil. And let these concepts become better known through examples.

For the zeal for the faith

10.1. The barbarians who fight us do so because they are actually fighting our faith. Because if we believed in the same [God] as them, then they would not fight us. It is terrible that the barbarians are fighting us to the

---

24 ἐκβησόμενον, from ἐκβαίνω: (metaph.) come out, turn out, to be fulfilled, of prophecies and so on.
25 ὁμοφύλους: of the same race or stock.

death for the faith, while at the same time we neglect to defend our own, discounting the insult to our God. Because the sides of Christ were speared for our salvation, so will we ignore His wounds? Our Lord died for us, will we not die for Him? **2.** Yes, we should do that, and with great pleasure. How could it be otherwise? Men give their lives for other men, so how can we fear death for the sake of our God? Who among you can show so much indifference and baseness, so that he is defeated in his zeal for his faith by the barbarians, to be ridiculed by them, rather than admired?

For the fatherland

11.1. By performing these actions for the benefit of the fatherland, to which we owe so much, such as our progress and upbringing, but also to our parents, children and siblings, how could we honour it worthily, if we did not endanger our property, our toil, but also our own lives, which, after all, come from it? Because nothing can compare to her graces. **2.** Indeed, given that we cannot do anything commendable enough as a token of gratitude, we will not neglect those to whom the corresponding act can be attributed, especially when, as a mother opens her arms and embraces us, welcomes us and implores us to take revenge on her behalf.[26]

For the love for our compatriots

12. The enemies, barbarians thought they might be, are still following the rules of nature and they fight for each other with great self-sacrifice, and do so even when they know they cannot rely on numbers or power.[27] We, on the other hand, who have a sufficient number of soldiers, but also remarkable power and, in addition, the love of God and the insatiable love for our

---

26 The comparison of the homeland with the mother figure is noteworthy here. The author of the text seeks to urge his audience to fight with the greatest heroism in favour of their homeland, as if they were going to do it for a member of their family. In this case, the mother is perhaps the person in whose defence the author believes that the fighters will fight with greater zeal. Homeland is, according to the author, responsible for the upbringing to the same degree as the family. In this way, he seeks to instil in the soldiers a sense of mental connection with the state entity they are called upon to defend. It is not something vague but rather something very specific, their own family. In the Later Roman world, a similar approach, of identification of the city with the earth, is followed by one of the main representatives of the Second Sophistic, Aelius Aristides in his *Praise of Rome* (W. Dindorf, *Aristides*, vol. 1 [Leipzig: Reimer, 1829 (repr. Hildesheim: Olms, 1964)], 321–70). See also Eramo (2010), 135 (n. 47), for further discussion and parallels from antiquity on the connection between homeland/*polis* and maternal figure.

27 δυνάμει, from δύναμις: strength, power, force for war.

people, how can we not fight for each other, when if we do not fight we and our families will suffer ruin,[28] how will we be able to sustain them all harmoniously, if not everyone is able to participate in the war on his own?

For the punishment of evildoers

13. Certainly, everything that we have suffered in the past from the enemies does not escape your memory. Nor were they so insignificant that they could be forgotten. It is terrible to tolerate the injustices of your enemies without defending yourself, without seeking revenge for the insults you have suffered. Because the more we tolerate their insults, the more we attract them to continue to come against us.

14.1. What is useful is achieved in three ways, from the soul, from the body, and from external elements. When I say from the soul, I refer to what improves the soul; from the body refers to what improves the body; the external elements mean wealth, fame and the like. **2.** The useful can be either necessary or beneficial. I call necessary what is life-saving when it exists and harmful when it is missing, for example the trees in the mountains are necessary not only for the city, as fuel for fire, which is one of the most necessary things, but also for the enemies at the same time, so that they will not capture the lumber and use it for the construction of stone-throwers and other siege engines to destroy the wall. Useful is something that, though not necessarily necessary, helps to have something necessary or something correspondingly useful. **3.** But sometimes the useful can become necessary, when the necessary cannot be achieved without it; for example, when fruits are useful to those who have grain, but if they lack the latter, then the fruits become necessary. **4.** Therefore, when there is a need to urge to war, it should be mentioned that it is not only useful, but also necessary. When Demosthenes was writing to the Athenians that it would be useful for them to ally with the Olynthians, in order to convince them that an alliance had to be made he added that "rather, it is necessary." **5.** The security of the present goods is therefore useful, but also the hope for obtaining future ones, as well as the relief from the present sufferings, but also the avoidance of any future ones. Likewise, the damage to the goods of the present is harmful, as it is the failure to acquire new goods in the future, as well as the continuation of the present evils but also the failure to anticipate possible future risks. It therefore happens that these elements derive from either doing or not doing something, especially in the present discussion, from the decision to fight or not to do it. **6.** Even these concepts become more familiar to us using

---

28 φθαρησόμεθα, from φθείρομαι: suffer ruin, damage.

examples, such as "war is more frightening to those who are inexperienced, but it is coveted for those who have already been recruited for battle, and it is also a hope of salvation for those who have suffered the injustices of the enemies. The fact that this war is useful to us, I believe that none of you ignores that. In fact, how could we defend ourselves, our homes, our cities and our territory in any other way?" **7.** It is useful to have in mind what is obvious, so that no one among us can ignore that it is also useful. And that it is absolutely necessary to have the intention to draw the sword, to have a warlike disposition and to move against the enemies. In fact, if we choose to do so with courage, then we will be better in every way, and we will be able to maintain the goods we already have, such as women, and children, and the goods the land offers us and other similar things, and in fact not only will we gain more through the spoils of the enemies, but also freely from our own possessions. On the other hand, we will shake off those evils that we already suffer from the enemies, so we will not have to suffer any more. Because the one who has been defeated [in war] tries to avoid war even more and to keep away from the same calamities and the same dangers, in which he had fallen in the past. **8.** If we now try to avoid battle against enemies that are already arrayed against us, then not only will we lose what we already have, but we will also lose hope of gaining more goods in the future. In fact, other afflictions will follow besides these, such as the captivity of women and children, the desertion of fields and famine, the complete destruction of cities, but also everything else that the enemies can do if we allow them. **9.** That is why we must hurry, before we have a taste of these calamities, to rush against the enemies, before they are even prepared. And this will not be just for the sake of gaining an advantage, it is essential. In fact, not only will we put our enemies to flight, but we will also ensure that our men take [good] courage,[29] which further builds up[30] victory.

15.1. Therefore, based on the points we have already talked about, not only the need to wage war is developed,[31] but also all the rest through which the war is brought to a successful conclusion.[32] These are five in number: preparation of weapons, training in the tactics of war, bravery, endurance of pain, and obedience to the rulers. Each of them is advantageous. **2.** Some of them are preparatory and we should make more use of them when we are safe, while others should be used when war is imminent, and for the reasons we have resorted to it.

---

29 θαρσῆσαι, from θαρσέω: to be of good courage, take courage, take heart for.
30 ἐργάζεται, from ἐργάζομαι: work, labour.
31 κατασκευάζεται, from κατασκευάζω: (in Logic) to construct an argument.
32 κατορθοῦται, from κατορθόω: to accomplish successfully, bring to a successful issue.

16. Perhaps one could consider that the things that cause some kind of pleasure are also useful. Among the things that cause pleasure are: the thoughts that bring joy, the sight of beautiful things, in terms of smell the ones that smell nice, in terms of touch the things that are smooth and soft, in terms of taste those that are sweet for some, but for others something different[33] and, to put it simply, whatever kind of preferences anyone has in terms of food and drink. For such things, the description is useful, one that satisfies a desire even before it is really satisfied. For example, when we talk about the land, that it is full of fruit, fertile, flowing with drinking water, open to breezes, shaded by flowering trees with dense foliage, rich in fruits of all kinds, bees that constantly produce honey from the flowers, swarms of melodious birds imitating the craft[34] of Orpheus. Thus, we talk about a city in the same way, how beautiful it is and how it has all kinds of luxuries,[35] et cetera.

17.1. The possible can be either difficult or simple. The difficult thing is what is achieved with great effort either due to lack of expenditures,[36] or due to another corresponding lack, while it becomes easy when none of them is missing. Still, here too we must show, just like we tried before to show that the useful can be necessary, that the possible is easy and that it does not take much effort to achieve the result. For instance: **2.** "It may seem difficult to conquer a city by attacking through the walls. On the other hand, I guess there is nothing easier than destroying the walls of a city, with the help of stone-throwers and other siege engines. Sometimes, the besieged citizens will surrender before the engines are even used, fearing for their lives."

18.1. As with the useful, the glorious is likewise divided into three parts: the soul,[37] the physical, and the external. As for the soul, it is courage – because that is the most glorious thing, for the body there is strength and beauty, while for the external things it is the social advancement[38] and power. **2.** Just like the useful, likewise the glorious is divided according to what one does or does not do against the enemies. For example, if we fight, then yes, we will uphold the glory we already have, but we will add even more. If some kind of ill repute[39] accompanies[40] us from the past, then we will get rid of it, while the chance of developing a bad reputation will not

---

33 ἕτερα, from ἕτερος: one or the other of two, other things of like kind.
34 τέχνην: an art, craft, trade.
35 τρυφή: luxuriousness, wantonness.
36 ἀνάλωμα: expenditure, cost.
37 ψυχή: breath, the soul, mind, the life, spirit, Lat. *anima.*
38 προύχουσαι, from προέχω: to be the first (of rank).
39 ἀδοξία: ill repute, contempt.
40 προλαβόντων, from προλαμβάνω: to be contained in advance.

bear fruit either. On the contrary, if we do not fight, then whatever glory we already have will be fleeting,[41] and the one we are seeking after will not come, the possible ill repute from the past will go on, while more will be added in the future. **3.** So the glorious should be elaborated according to the useful, not only from the positions that have already been formulated, but also from arguments and other.

19. In addition to these, there are other points, which we ourselves have found out[42] and which, based on the subject, we have called fake, that is, completely fabricated arguments. For example, the general may tell the army that he spoke to the emperor on its [the army's] behalf, and that in these words the emperor responded favourably to the army, or something fictitious (false), like an official from the emperor's entourage could say to have written letters to the general, which would urge the army for the impending war. Further, one could persuade the deserters (of the enemy) to report that there is wealth in the city or in a foreign region, information that otherwise could hardly be trusted. These conventions can be more easily understood through examples.[43]

41 ἀπολεῖται, from ἀπόλλυμι: lost, to be undone.
42 προσεξευρήκαμεν, from προσεξευρίσκω: to find out or devise besides.
43 Agathias, a sixth-century Byzantine historian, gives an excellent example of the use of a fabricated letter and news to animate the troops. Among other things, Agathias gives us information about the Great War of Lazika that lasted from AD 541 until 566. Romans and Persians fought hard for the occupation of Lazika, and the incident that concerns us happened during the years 555–556. Martinus, who served at the time as *magister militum per Armenian* and thus commander-in-chief of the Roman armies in the area, faced a difficult situation, as he was besieged in the city of Phasis by significantly superior Persian forces under Nacharagan. The morale of the besieged Roman troops was low, so Martinus resorted to the following trick to boost it. He presented to the assembled army that news had come in the form of a letter from a man who pretended to be the imperial messenger. The letter said that reinforcements from Istanbul would soon arrive in the besieged city. Therefore, the general not only tried to raise the morale of his soldiers but at the same time encouraged them to show greater vigilance, achieving victory over the enemies before the new troops arrived and possibly sharing the spoils with them. The Roman troops then drove the Persians away, inflicting heavy casualties on them. For Martinus, a seasoned soldier who also fought in Africa against the Vandals and in Italy against the Goths, see PLRE *Martinus 2* in J. R. Martindale, *The Prosopography of the Later Roman Empire: Volume 3B, AD 527–641* (Cambridge: Cambridge University Press, 1992), 839–48. For the war in Lazika during Justinian I's rule, see O. Mazal, *Justinian I und seine Zeit: Geschichte und Kultur des Byzantinischen Reiches im 6. Jahrhundert* (Köln and Weimar: Böhlau Verlag, 2001), 118–21, and of course the excellent study by Greatrex and Lieu (Geoffrey Greatrex and Samuel N. C. Lieu, *The Roman Eastern Frontier and the Persian Wars (Part II, 363–630 ad)* (London: Routledge, 2002). For Agathias' original account, see the two-volume set (edition and translation in English) by Frendo, esp. pp. 90–9 (translation) (J. Frendo (ed.), *Agathias: The Histories* [Berlin and New York: De Gruyter, 1975]).

20.1. "Oftentimes when hearing your words, with which you demonstrated your propensity for war, my soul rejoiced, and finding myself together with the other generals, when they exalted their soldiers, I too, boasting about mine [you] argued that just as practice makes good speech, so war reveals the worthy soldier. **2.** Sometimes, I also carried back[44] your own speeches to the ears of the emperor himself, just as if you were present and exposed them to him. **3.** For how long will we be indifferent? For how long will we avoid war? For how long will we postpone the inevitable war? For how long will not only our compatriots but also our enemies depict us as cowards and consider us to behave in an effeminate[45] way? Because we can no longer tolerate to do and listen to these things. And if others happen to want to avoid war, we willingly want to take their place, for the glory of God, the boast of the emperor and the salvation of our compatriots." **4.** The king's soul rejoiced in hearing these words, how could it be otherwise? Moreover, he said, "many claimed a lot, which through their actions turned out to be lies. Hence, if your army shows its worth in the war, then we will show our gratitude to it. **5.** As the time for the trial/struggle[46] [of weapons] has come, and what you were seeking you finally found, with your actions show your willingness, your bravery, your perseverance and your other virtues, through which a war brings glory and success."

Other made-up arguments

21.1. "One time, a dinner was held in the presence of the sovereign, and the guests were generals; I was among them. While some of the generals boasted about their achievements, I intervened in the conversation with the following words: **2.** "It is said that Phokion's wife,[47] when asked why she does not wear as much jewellery as other women, replied: 'my jewellery is my husband's success.' For exactly the same reason, if someone would ask me, wanting to know about my jewellery, I would answer that they are the successes of my soldiers. Because they choose and consider a pleasure the things [of war] that bring fear to most people. **3.** Therefore, see how

---

44 ἀνήγαγον, from ἀνάγω: lead up from a lower place to a higher, refer a claimant.
45 γυναικώδεις: woman-like, womanish.
46 ἀγώνων, from ἀγών: gathering, assembly, place of contest, battle, action, struggle for life and death.
47 The reference to Fokion's wife shows, once again, the deep knowledge of the ancient literature that the author of the text had. This time he draws an example from Plutarch and the Life of Fokion and, more specifically, from 19.4 (K. Ziegler, *Plutarchi vitae parallelae*, vol. 2.1, 2nd ed. [Leipzig: Teubner, 1964], esp. Ch.19.4). See also Eramo (2010), 144 (n. 59), on further discussion on the other uses of Fokion's wife as example of modesty.

much we appreciate your virtues, how much we emphasize your successes even before the emperor. And we will boast about them even more if you help each other and you join forces to gain more glory in the coming war. **5.** Doing what? Going forward, pushing[48] each other against the barbarians, presenting your weapons, fighting bravely for victory, hoping for the crowns of glory after the victory, the applause and all the relevant advantages, which bring eternal pleasure and enjoyment."

22.1. Such arguments are even more useful when we also come up with letters through which the emperor is supposed to address to the army. Something like this, for example: **2.** "Men, brothers, soldiers: Many times I felt that your general was proud of your actions, and I rejoiced too. In fact, nothing can delight the heart of an emperor more than the good performance of one of his subjects and the faith displayed through his deeds. **3.** Accordingly, if the words of your general ring true, now is the time to prove it through this struggle/fight. Remember the love I have for you. **4.** Indeed, for this very reason I wish to consider myself a soldier, to call myself your comrade-in-arms, although I do not put off[49] my paternal feelings[50] [to you]. Indeed, even if I exhort you as your emperor, at the same time I exhort you as a father and encourage you as a brother, not because I am any better than you,[51] but so that you may become the fear of our enemies, and the reason for the salvation of our people, and to be on the lips of the people, not only for your exploits, but also for the fact that you suffered and you came back with wounds, which fill me with more joy even than the glow of shining gemstones." **5.** (8) And again from the general: "Such are the words of our emperor! How can I respond to that, as a grateful servant of the emperor to his fellow servants or as a soldier to his fellow soldiers?" **6.** "Of course, all other rewards are good, which come from the hands of the emperor, but there is nothing more important and beautiful than a word of love, which comes from the soul of the ruler that is burning with such feelings for his army." **7.** Therefore, having set aside his royal status and the absolute power he possesses, he speaks to us as if we were his legitimate children and calls upon us to fight for our salvation, how useful it is therefore for us to welcome his words and honour them by faithfully following the instructions given to us? **8.** "For this reason alone we will be rewarded with additional rewards, not to make him gain more, but to better ourselves, so that they deserve royal gratitude and reward."

---

48 συνωθοῦντες, from συνωθέω: force together, compress forcibly.
49 ἀναβάλλομαι, from ἀναβάλλω: put back, put off.
50 προσηγορίαν: friendly greeting, familiarity.
51 Alternatively: "not because I have anything more than you do."

23. Beneficial[52] for the war are not only these made up speeches, but also other things, such as forcing some of the enemy's deserters to tell our own during the siege that the besiegers or the besieged lack the necessary food, or that there is gold in the city, and silver and other precious goods, which the soldiers long for.

24.1. Such positions therefore become even more elaborate in speech with the use of arguments and syllogisms, as they develop, but at the same time with their connection to reality. For example, the letters allegedly sent by the emperor seem real because of the couriers that bring them and because they bear all the signs that characterize an imperial letter; enemy intelligence, in other words news about the cowardice of the enemies, or how few in number they are, or how rich their city is, appears legitimate because it derives from deserters. **2.** In fact, in some cases one can check the veracity of the intelligence against reality, for instance the wealth of a city is apparent in the buildings, in their multiple storeys, in the columns that are higher than the walls, whereas the lack of manpower is made obvious by how few the defenders of the city are. The arguments for our discussion so far are rather sufficient.

25.1. Every argument can be drawn either from reality: from a person, or from time, or from a place or from something made up. **2.** It is said that an argument comes from an event, when the structure of the argument itself is based on an event. From a person, as Hermogenes himself claims, when it comes from a person. The same when it comes from time, place, or another occasion. However, a made up argument is one that starts from a made up fact and we end up elaborating the rest of our position/argument [from that fact]. **3.** And to make this context even more understandable, let us consider what is lawful as the main point. For example, a deserter should be subject to capital punishment. That is why, the argument that comes from reality is this: the law is not only good but it is also the most useful thing, while when it comes from a person it will be as follows: "It suits us to obey the law, and to convince ourselves that we must always act in accordance with the requirements of the law."

25a. The arguments coming from persons can be drawn from the religion, from the mode of life, and from the slander of the enemy army. From religion if they are characterized as pious or ungodly. From the way of life if they are virtuous or vice versa. From the slander of the opposing army, if for example that they are well equipped, that they are many, that they are capable of war, but also the opposite, that is, that they are few, unarmed, inexperienced in war. These arguments taken by the enemy himself are also clear and we will present them below with examples.

---

52 λυσιτελεῖ: useful, profitable, advantageous.

From religion

26.1. "And I really wonder if someone, having seen how impious our enemies are, is not in a hurry to fight them with all his might. They have stripped off[53] God or they are fighting against God. In any case, even if there are no others willing to fight against them, it is absolutely necessary for us to do so, who are characterized by piety and are always protectors of the law."

From the mode of life

26.2. "Seeing how [the enemies] live (i.e. their way of life), how rude they are, how unjust they are, how completely foreign to the truth, I would say that you are even more ready to fight against them. In fact, one is led to oppose something that is contrary to one's own beliefs (or way of life), in order to despise[54] those who follow it[55] [live contrary to its principles] and in the end to fight them as enemies."

From the slander of the enemy army

26.3. "Many of those who have deserted to us say that the enemy has gathered farmers and other craftsmen, hardly armed at all, to wage war against us."

From [the right] time

27.1. "And for us now is the time to rush into the impending conflict. To seize the opportunity for salvation, which if we lose will cause us harm."

From the place

27.2. "Do you not see what the battlefield is like? How much does it help us, and at the same time how much does it impair our enemies?"

From the cause

28.1. Arguments drawn from the cause are taken mainly from the past, but many times the preamble can be made with arguments from the present and from the future.

---

53 γυμνούς: naked, unclad, stripped of a thing.
54 βδελύσσεται, from βδελύσσομαι: to be loathsome.
55 κεκτημένους, from κτάομαι: procure for oneself, get, acquire, have in store, have in hand.

From the past, in this way[56]

28.2. Brothers, fellow soldiers, I believe that no one among you forgets the suffering caused to us by our enemies and that it is absolutely necessary that we take revenge on them for all their insults. In fact, just as it is not lawful to punish an innocent person, so it is not possible to leave a guilty person unpunished, ignoring those who have been wronged.

From the present, such as[57]

28.3. "Even if there was no sign of hostility on the part of the enemy, we should not be complacent, but suspect future events. In fact, the opposite could be due to misinformation. But since now we see them seeking our death and standing with arms against us, how can we not take up arms against them willingly and show them that they do not fight against women, but against men who boast of their military achievements."

From the future, such as

28.4. "However, my fellow soldiers, even if we were going to the impending war for something else, such as the glory, then to enjoy our own goods or not to face in the future the bitterness of their loss, that is why we must be ready and act accordingly. For who does not know that, if we defeat the enemies, not only will we preserve the goods that belong to us, but also at the same time we will acquire what belongs to the enemies. On the other hand, if we renounce the war, we may temporarily save our lives by choosing to flee, but soon all together and our families will be destroyed."

From the fabrications,[58] such as

28.5. "Should this ever happen, what would you say? Will we not repent this afterwards? Will we not pull and cut our hair as a sign of mourning? Will we not wet our cheeks with even hotter tears? Because which soul bears the loss of both his wife and his children and the desolation of his house? Will we not say later that thousands of deaths should we have suffered, rather than see this, rather than suffer this? But what is the point of delivering

---

56 οὕτως: in this way.
57 οἷον: such as, as for instance, like.
58 πλαστῶν, from πλαστός: (metaph.) fabricated, forged, hypothetical case.

these speeches in a dramatic way after the misfortune, when weeping will be useless?" And for these arguments, what we have already said is enough. **29.1.** To the same extent that these arguments help to further elaborate the points [of the discourse], as we have already mentioned, so too the exposition[59] prepares the argument. **2.** The exposition is the comparison[60] of a certain fact with the argument that has already been put forward. If this is drawn from the same genre,[61] it is called an example, such as: "let us not give money to Dionysius, because when Peisistratos took them, he became a tyrant." On the other hand, if it is drawn from a similar genre,[62] then it is called a parable.[63] For example: "we have to defend ourselves against the enemies, as the cranes do." **3.** We draw the examples from greater/stronger, equal or weaker [situations]; for an example of the weaker, if the Romans said: "let us imitate the Athenians"; on the other hand, for an example of the greater/stronger, if the Athenians said: "let us imitate the Romans"; while for an example of the equals, this would be if the Athenians said "let us imitate the Lacedemonians." **4.** It is also possible to construct part of the speech not only with examples, but also with parables, such as: "not only human beings, in whom we find the greatest potential, do this, but even animals themselves; for when oxen, horses and sheep are about to encounter dangerous predators, they hide the weakest parts of their body by uniting in formation, some show their horns, others stretch their hind legs and others show their teeth. Likewise, the birds try to protect themselves from danger by thickening their formation, so that eventually they choke[64] what is chasing them." **5.** Alternatively: "Oh, don't you see that too? Each thread by itself is weak and breaks whenever one wants to break it, but when many threads are intertwined into a single one, then even many people working together cannot break it with the same ease."

30. Once again, examples can be drawn from the achievements of the audience, from those of the ancestors of the audience, but also from the achievements of others.

The achievements of the audience

31. "One could exhort you with the same actions that you did in previous military operations, even before we make our speech. I agree with that

---

59 ἐργασία: work, business, exposition.
60 ἀφομοίωσις: making like, comparison.
61 ὁμοειδῶν: of the same species or kind.
62 ὁμοιοειδῶν: of like form, species or kind.
63 παραβολή: a parable, that is, a fictitious narrative by which some religious or moral lesson is conveyed.
64 ἀποπνίγουσιν, from ἀποπνίγω: choke, throttle, cut off, kill.

myself, and for that reason let us leave aside the successes of others. I am here to remind you of your own successes, the ones you achieved during this war, and the reason why you are admired by all. Therefore, I urge you to be motivated by yourselves, giving another proof of your worth in the war, so that they admire you even more."

The achievements of the ancestors of the audience

32. "Our ancestors of old, those who once achieved many great successes, are still praised today for their skills in arms. May we do likewise, following in their footsteps, pursue glory, in order to reach it and be crowned with similar achievements. You see that, as I told you from the beginning, I am addressing you as your father, and to you, my true children, I wish your salvation. Therefore, you too hasten,[65] along with your father, to call upon the heavenly powers, to show in battle the same strength, intention, courage and bravery, to do the same feats that transformed the Romans from a small nation to a great one, as they attacked the land of enemies and made it their own. That is why they are still praised for these achievements. So we too must follow the path of their conquests, to become equally worthy of praise."

The achievements of others

33. "It should not have been necessary, O Romans, to try to imitate the acts of bravery of others, but instead to strive to be role models for others through our virtues. However, since we see that others have to show achievements without fear of misfortune or danger, either for glory or for self-interest, how could we also choose not to do the same, in order to be worthy of glory much more than they?"

34. One should avoid drawing examples from opponents. Praising the opponents carries the risk of causing cowardice in our soldiers. However, if one wants to do so, let him praise the warlike disposition of the adversaries, showing their actions, for example: "see our enemies and what things they have been able to achieve in the past." For the most part, however, he should calumniate[66] them, such as: "surely, although they do not have the necessary numbers, they have courage. Because they have claimed to present as an achievement only their intention for the fight." Thus much in relation to the exposition.[67]

---

65 σπεύσατε, from σπεύδω: set going, urge on, hasten.
66 ἐνδιαβάλλων, from ἐνδιαβάλλω: calumniate.
67 According to the author, the general should avoid praising the warlike virtues of the opponents, as this could have a negative effect on the morale of his own army. Instead, the

35.1. Now we will talk about syllogisms: this is essentially a juxtaposition of an exposition and an argument, which brings together the probable with the argument, an argument that is derived from an individual, such as: "it is good to fight to protect your compatriots," then adding "as all other foreign nations do." If we say: "but they are barbarians, while on the contrary we behave, as we should, properly both in life and with the word," this is what we call a syllogism. **2.** Likewise, we could make another argument that is derived from an action, "we should be vigilant," using a similar example: "since many other animals do," and add, "of course, they are irrational[68] beings, while we participate having used our reason." **3.** This example, or more precisely the comparison, is called a syllogism. In addition, it is possible, when the argument is missing, to compare the exposition with the main argument,[69] that it is fair for this to happen, for example: "this is not only done by the Greeks, but also by the barbarians," then this syllogism creates comparison between these elements/points. **4.** Among the comparisons, the most likely is the one that establishes the comparison starting from the weaker, and then what concerns the equal, and more rarely when it comes to the greater/stronger. In practice, it is difficult to imitate someone much better. One army is better than another either because of its numerical strength, or because of the weapons it is armed with, or because of its experience, or for some other reason, due to which men generally prove victorious in war.

36.1. So we have covered thus far the chapters, and the arguments, the expositions and the syllogisms, and how each one is used. Therefore, what has been said is enough. However, how all this can be combined,[70] we will show through an example. **2.** "As I have loved and protected you, my good and valiant comrades-in-arms, in the same way that a father does, it is impossible for you to fully learn it from anyone else. Because you have to remember that while you were sleeping at night, I was awake, and when you were resting from your daily toils, I struggled even harder. What

---

general should raise the morale of the army by referring to the elements that made the opponents inferior. For example, the description of Procopius, Belisarius' speech to the Roman troops during the campaign and battle at Daras, is quite vivid. Belisarius tells his soldiers that the Persian infantry consists of villagers without discipline, without special warlike virtues (τὸ γὰρ πεζὸν ἅπαν οὐδὲν ἄλλο ἢ ὅμιλός ἐστιν ἀγροίκων οἰκτρῶν), so that if the Romans follow the orders faithfully, the victory will inevitably be theirs. See G. Wirth (post J. Haury), *Procopii Caesariensis opera omnia*, vol. 1–2 (Leipzig: Teubner, 1905), esp. *De Bellis*, book 1, ch. 14. For further discussion on similar examples, see also Eramo (2010), 153 (n. 88).

68 ἄλογος: without λόγος, irrational.
69 κεφάλαιον: chief or main point.
70 συμπλέκεται: (Pass.) to be intertwined, locked together, combine notions logically under one term.

was I doing? I was looking out for your interests, now walking around the palisade, now inspecting the ditches, and the like respectively, taking care of your safety. Why [was I doing] all this? To prevent the enemies from attacking the army at night, after having escaped our attention. **3.** For these reasons, it is necessary for you, just as children do, to follow our commands and understand that these deeds are your salvation. For I am fully convinced that, if you listen to this speech with the same goodwill[71] and go immediately and take action, everything will turn out well for you. **4.** And we, after being decorated with this victory against the barbarians, will benefit in many ways and rewards, and we will be the object of admiration by all. **5.** That is why I do not advise you on something that is unknown to you, but on the reasons for which we raise an army and on everything that the soldier prepares for, even without being forced to do so, see for example, our enemies, as they come against us, perhaps been forced to, despite their individual will, so let us put aside all our other activities and be vigilant about the conflict. Convinced of your worth in arms, I come with joy to exhort you to war. **6.** It is therefore necessary to put aside any delay and laziness and not to wait for the enemies, but with greater courage to rush against them and engage in war. **7.** And indeed, many times when the holy Gospels were recited we have heard Christ saying more or less the following: 'Thus I confess that you are my disciples, when you love one another,' and elsewhere: 'there is no greater act of love, from giving one's life for someone close to him.' **8.** So if we too take part in the teachings of God with our faith, let us love our brothers and sisters, and let us give our lives for one another and our co-religionists, so that by our actions we may become true disciples of Christ. **9.** But even for those who do not understand the divine law exactly like that, because Christ prevented Peter from using his knife, we should resort to the use of weapons as a last recourse, for the common good and in exceptional circumstances. **10.** The laws are good, and above all the laws that come from God himself, and we all strive to obey them. Indeed, what could be more useful to people than the law of God? A law gave value to the Maccabees, a law glorified the children, and even the fire showed respect for those who keep the Mosaic Laws, and enveloped the enemies before turning them to ashes, a law makes the beast behave calmly, so to speak, so that it respects the law-abiding. The Chaldean king and an army obeying the orders of tyrants knew this. **11.** If beasts have respect for the law-abiding man, and when fire envelops and imprisons those who offend the Holy, we who consider ourselves guardians of the Divine Laws, how could we remain indifferent to our God being insulted?"

---

71 *προθέσεως*: statement of a case, theme, thesis, goodwill.

37.1. "Perhaps you, friends and brothers, have forgotten my efforts and anxieties, but I can never forget your virtues, that is, submission, discipline, and self-sacrifice. **2.** Indeed, I have in mind, and have not forgotten, your past achievements in this war, during which I gave you a command and you immediately put it to action – because we must admit the truth – and for that you claimed the greatest achievements at the time. **3.** That is why I have come to urge you to the present war. Because I know very well that if you listen to me now, you will be distinguished[72] more than before in the fight against the enemies. **4.** It is therefore necessary to explain and present our positions. The enemies will come against us and no one will be able to escape, neither our cities, nor our fields, nor our people. **5.** We must therefore understand that the anxiety of our people does not come from the fear of our enemies, but from our reluctance to fight. **6. (5).** So come on, let us cast out this fear, do what is useful to all of us and prepare for the coming war. Because it is fair to us but also a cause of salvation for our people. **7. (6).** We know indeed, very well, that of all the values that improve life, none can be compared to justice. And for these reasons we must honour it and fight the enemies, firstly because they are infidels who insult our faith, secondly because they have repeatedly attacked our country (even now if they avoid this war, they will soon wish to attack us again and they will come out against our country), thirdly, out of our love of one another[73] – for they have indeed fallen against us and therefore we must defeat them, not only for our own self-interest, but because we do it for our compatriots – fourthly, because we have already suffered so much from them and it is necessary to punish them for their injustice. Indeed, everyone does that. **8. (7).** It is proper for us to preserve justice, both because we are Romans and because we emulate the valour of our fathers: many times against the same enemies they did not remain indifferent to what was happening, but they campaigned[74] and punished them in an even harsher way. **9. (8).** If those who sought justice against their enemies have gained so much glory, even though they were previously humble, how could we not seek justice with even more zeal from the enemies, for all that they have inflicted on us, since we have the force that is no different from that of our ancestors?"

38. So we should use as our main argument what comes from the fatherland and is even more useful to us, as it gives us the reason why it is necessary to fight for it [the fatherland], recognizing the goods that come from her:

---

72 εὐδοκιμήσετε, from εὐδοκιμέω: to be of good repute, highly esteemed, popular.

73 ἀλλήλων: of one another, to one another, one another.

74 στρατευόμενοι, from στρατεύω: advance with an army or fleet, wage war, have been soldiers.

"Indeed, she gave birth to us, raised us, gave us the best possible education, and, along with all other goods, gave us the inheritance of our ancestors." **39.1.** "It is a great evil for people to be deprived of their property, especially when they lose their rulers and fall into a state of slavery, or even lose their lives. **2.** That is why we must defend ourselves against those who dare to cause such suffering, unless one wants to suffer all these calamities without reaction. For everyone knows how many and what kind of damage our enemies have done to us. **3.** They burned our trees, stole our animals and oxen, and killed many of our own people. **4.** For all these reasons, I call on you to fight together against the enemies. Because this is appropriate, as it is useful for us, but also for all those who have suffered because of the enemies, and no one could remain idle while enduring such calamities. **5.** Because as for the others, such as the lawful, the just, the possible, the glorious, many overlook them sometimes, but no one can overlook the useful. **6.** I also see the field of the coming battle, which will help us in case of difficulty – indeed we have cities around us that could welcome us if we had to escape in case of defeat, but on the other hand, if we win, then none of our enemies could escape, and so I become even more eager for the impending war. **7. (6).** Because the help that a battlefield can offer to those who know how to use it is great. **8. (6).** The mob of the Scythians and the king of the Persians know this, the former having defeated superior enemies due to the battlefield, and the latter having been defeated by inferior opponents, then being forced to kneel and beg for freedom. **9. (7).** If, then, the Scythians seize such courage[75] by trusting exclusively in the battlefield, how much better would we be than the enemies, having so much power and apparatus of arms on top of the strength that the battlefield gives us?"

More examples about the useful

The preparation of weapons

40.1. Since, O Romans, our enemies are not by nature likely to remain idle, we in turn must be ready to fight them, first of all by taking care of the necessary preparations for war, and preparing the necessary weapons, according to what has been determined, so that when the time comes none of you would be lacking them. **2.** It is good, indeed, to have prepared weapons in advance, without which it would be impossible to fight, because weapons help you face the battle with more courage. **3.** For as the plough is to the farmer, the digger and the mattock to the planter, the oars and the anchor to

---

75 θαρρήσαντες, from θαρσέω: to be of good courage, feel confidence against.

the sailors, so for the soldier these are the sword, the spear and the shield, and anything else we use to protect ourselves and fight against our enemies.[76] **4.** For indeed, even if they live in a different way, they are just as diligent in preparing for war, so that they do not consider themselves inferior to their potential enemies, like us, how will we face the enemies without weapons, how do we do it if we have no other hope of living beyond fighting?

The training in war tactics

41.1. "Training improves a lot of practical activities, such as painting or sculpture, and so with exactly the same logic success in war comes from constant practice. **2.** In fact, there is nothing good that has not been studied in advance, as practice is the main path for those who want to win, and no one, if properly prepared, can fail. For this reason, before the track and field events the corresponding preparations are made, before the equestrian exercises the corresponding study takes place, and the like. It would therefore be terrible to practice in these areas, and give no thought to the exercises for war. **3.** This main point may also be used for the study of battle tactics, and especially when the time of war is fast approaching, for example: 'Many times in the heat of battle many jump in front of the phalanx, breaking the formation. On the one hand I praise their intention, but on the other I do not approve of such actions. First of all, because they break the formation, which

---

76 As Eramo (2010), 165–6 (n. 112) rightly points out, the author emphasizes the value of weapons as a means of defence against any threat. The struggle of the Byzantines is defensive and justified against an unjust enemy, but even if it is aggressive, then it aims to restore an injustice, retaliation for a hostile act. E. Luttwak, in his work *The Grand Strategy of the Byzantine Empire* (Cambridge: The Belknap Press of Harvard University Press, 2011), 416, among other things states the following aspect of the Byzantine's *operational code*: "Avoid war by every possible means in all possible circumstances, but always act as if it might start at any time. Train both individual recruits and complete formations intensively, exercise units against each other, prepare weapons and supplies to be ready for battle at all times – but do not be eager to fight. The highest purpose of maximum combat readiness is to increase the probability of not having to fight at all." Thus, according to the Syrianos magistros, the soldiers should be well acquainted with their art (of war), because well-trained fighters are in themselves a threat to any potential enemy, ensuring peace without possible bloodshed. A poorly trained army is a motive for a potential enemy to attack without fear. Of course, the Byzantines had other means of preventing war, such as bribery and turning their enemies to fight against each other. However, these practices were to some extent more effective before the rise of Islam and the great Arab conquests, as the war now had a different character, under the guise of the "Holy War." For these means, see Tilemachos Lounghis' recent study, "Alternative Means of Conflict Resolution," in: Yannis Stouraitis (ed.), *A Companion to the Byzantine Culture of War, ca. 300–1204* (Leiden: Brill, 2018), 196–226.

is useful when it is solid, and jump in front of their comrades, when standing next to them would have been more effective in warding off the formation of the enemy. Secondly, because they put themselves in a situation where they can get no help and end up getting killed. Thirdly, because on many occasions they become a cause of ruin for their other comrades-in-arms. **4.** For this reason, breaking formation and running in front of the phalanx is harmful, and often more dangerous than the action of the enemies themselves. It is therefore better to remain steadfast in our own lines and in the ranks where we have been placed, so that the phalanx is preserved solid and strong.'"

Bravery

42.1. Of the many things that cause happiness in life, the most important is courage, since through it we not only secure what belongs to us, but also at the same time we can harm what belongs to our enemies.

The endurance of pain[77]

42.2. "I consider it important that we warmly accept the pain of participating in war, especially the demonstration of endurance. **3.** Because it would be terrible, indeed, to engage lightly in battle and then easily retreat from it, causing the defeat and death of others, rather than bravely standing your ground with your weapons and courageously facing the battle."

The obedience to the commanders

43.1. "If ever there was a need for obedience to the commanders, O my friends, my children, my brothers, now is the time to do so willingly; for it is good to follow the commanders' orders. **2.** Because what they do, they do for the good of their subordinates. And what do they do? They stay alert, they worry, they see the problems of their subordinates and they treat them as their own, and before the others they are the ones who hurt along with the others and carry this pain in their hearts, as they are no different from our fathers. **3.** So it is good to obey their commands, as even bees do. In fact, bees have a rule not to leave the hive unless their king leaves first. **4.** And if the bees show such honour and obedience to their king, an insect, how much more obedience should you be expected to show to our orders, the more so since we always think and act for your own good?"

---

77 πόνων, from πόνος: physical pain; work, especially hard work; toil; stress; trouble; distress; suffering.

The study of the glorious

44.1. "That you are well disposed towards us, O good and brave army, following our orders and carrying them out with alacrity, I myself will testify to it and proclaim it everywhere, even if no one else admits it publicly. **2.** But how do you treat yourselves? Do you take care of yourselves, or have you surrendered to banquets and laziness? **3.** Absolutely not. And neither I nor anyone else can believe this, even if you remain silent. How could it be otherwise? It is clear that just like a father with his children, so am I happy with your joys, in pain with what upsets you, I feel what concerns you as my own problem. **4.** And what you have experienced is proof of this. I am referring to when we entered the battle at dusk and worked every night as if it was daytime, when you showed obedience and absolute discipline to us, considering fatigue as normal, as well as treating death as if it were as coveted as life, reasons why you receive recognition of your worth from everyone. **5.** Well, what I had advised you back then, I have come now to advise you again. And behold, here are our enemies. Although they seem to be ready to attack us, in reality they are probably afraid of us. **6.** And I assure you that I see them moving with great hesitation, as if motivated only by the fear of the whip. **7.** But with this spectacle, we march against them with greater courage, being on the right path to victory, under the guidance of God. At this point, we will put an end to the words, as you along with the general and with God's help take over the management of things. **8.** It is possible not only to prevail against the enemies in their present numbers, but to be able to repel them even if they had an even greater number of troops. **9.** It is not really the number of soldiers that brings victory, but bravery and the endurance of pain. Many examples of other people convince us of this, especially the Macedonians who destroyed Asia with 40,000 men, or the Athenians who faced a huge Persian army twice, destroying one and repulsing the other after causing them a large number of casualties. **10.** So, if the Athenians, with such small numbers and so limited a territory, achieved such great feats of courage, how much more appropriate would it be for us to stand against the enemies and to be a model of bravery for others, to be admired not only by our contemporaries, but by future generations as well?"

The study of the possible

45.1. "Once again I have before me the army of the Great King, but again I rejoice and I feel the flutter of hope and I become more cheerful[78] myself.

---

78 φαιδρότερος, from φαιδρός: bright, beaming, (metaph.) beaming with joy, bright, cheerful.

Because your achievements against the enemy that I have mentioned in the previous part of my speech, these achievements are repeated by the tongues of so many and in books, and not even the years could diminish their greatness. **2.** Therefore, even now, I am here to urge you on this war. Behold, the enemies approach, I do not know whether because they no longer remember their defeats in the past, or because they are unaware of our presence, or for some other reason, or because God blinds them and pushes them into our hands. **3.** Forward, my brave and beloved soldiers, come forward to fight the enemies, to fight them for many reasons, including glory, which is in fact closer to my heart, glory more than any other good. **4.** For men, nothing is more painful than the very pursuit of glory. Whatever they do, they do for glory. **5.** And what is worth more than anything else with a victory against the barbarians, when this effort and sympathy come through love for the compatriots? **6.** For her the donations, for her all the wreaths, for her all the awards, the honours, the triumphs, the epic chants, and everything else that makes life happier and the mouth of History open wide. **7.** Because of her, an Athenian man who had been taken prisoner by the Persians in a campaign was once asked by them what the Athenians meant by manliness.[79] Then the man asked for a torch, and when they gave it to him, he placed his right hand over the flame and held it until the flesh melted from the bone and fell to the ground. **8.** Once upon a time, the Persians mutilated and tortured their bodies, in order to present themselves as enemies of their own people before deserting to the enemies, some to be able to instil in them the feeling of cowardice, making them think of withdrawing, others so that during a siege they might set fire to the city, or open the gates, or run up to the battlements to help their own during the night battle. **9.** So if the Persians, barbarians though they are, dared to do such things in search of temporary glory and honour, how can we not fight to the last man, not only for a temporary glory, but also for immortality, for the sake of our compatriots and ourselves? **10.** Because as much as we differ from them in terms of the knowledge of what is good, that much more we also demand the pains that a war brings."

The study of the outcome of the battle

46.1. Some of us may think that if we win this war it will be absolutely useful for us, but if that does not happen, then it will be very destructive. I do not claim this thing, but that which is closer to the truth and most useful to everyone. **2.** What is that? The fact that, if we force our enemies to flee, then hardly any of them will be able to escape us. If, on the other hand, the

---

79 ἀνδρείαν, from ἀνδρεῖος: manly, masculine, strong, vigorous; in a bad sense, stubborn.

enemies manage to drive us away, then I know very well that our lands on the high mountains will immediately welcome us, while there will be men who will turn against the enemies and fight to conquer victory. Furthermore, our cities and villages will be able to avoid the possible sufferings of war. **3.** Therefore, as long as the favourable conditions remain, we should take advantage of them without hesitation. In fact, the present conditions all but shout at us to declare war. **4.** For the enemies' allies have moved away from them and the latter are plagued by internal problems, while on the contrary we are in complete concord[80] and have all the necessary supplies and everything else that is useful for a war. **5.** It is said that the Macedonian [Alexander the Great?] once, when asked how he was blessed with such good fortune, replied that he had not wasted time. **6.** So, if he, who over time increased and broadened his power, still needed more time for future enterprises, how can we not do everything at our disposal to make time before it passes, to wage war against our opponents? **7.** Or do you not see the statue that represents time, which can be grasped only when it passes in front of someone, while afterwards it is impossible?

47.1. Therefore, concerning the prelude, the preamble and the preface, as well as the preliminary exposition and proposition, what we have said so far is enough about how to build useful arguments for the proposed question. **2.** It should be noted, however, that there are instances when the development (the arguments) comes immediately after the position, especially when war is imminent. For example, if we say: "it is a law to fight for the homeland," then we add: "for both Telon the Athenian and Zopyros the Persian risked their lives, the former for his homeland, the latter for his fellow-soldiers." **3.** You should also know that, whenever the development is introduced after the position, the critical circumstances[81] are omitted[82] as arguments, while the burden falls on the syllogisms, since one or more comparisons are made in them; for instance, when, after bringing the example as to the lawful, that the Persians risked their lives for their country when necessary, we add: "barbarians though they are and sometimes forget their nature, but we consider the law to be the most beautiful thing we have, for which we are educated and want to maintain."

48. Sometimes, when time is if the essence, we leave out not only the arguments, but also the development and the syllogism, contenting ourselves only with the position. In particular, we can resort to the most convincing

---

80 ὁμόνοια: oneness of mind, unanimity, concord.

81 περιστατικά: of or in critical circumstances; (Rhet.) concerned with the circumstances of a case.

82 ἐκλείπω: leave out, pass over.

argument, for example: "fighting for our homelands is in accordance with the law, it is just, and it is useful, and so on."

49.1. Next, we will deal with the peroration[83] of all the above. We will have to resort again to the strongest of the previous arguments we have used in the previous parts, but not in the exact same way, as we will try to emphasize one particular thing, namely what is useful. **2.** Before, in the various arguments, we simply said that this and that will happen, but not in the peroration, since there we must emphasize to the listeners the causes of what will happen. **3.** For in this way, even more urgently, will we be able to persuade them to follow the orders, saying for example, "Do not allow, O Roman men, a barbaric sword to desecrate the tombs of your ancestors, or let your wives be made the property of other men because of your idleness, and your children the slaves of our enemies, who will drag them miserably into a foreign land, and they will be begging for a drop of water, or waiting to taste the leftovers from the table of the foreigners.[84] **4.** That is why we must consider the following: all this will not happen because of the power of the enemies, but because of our voluntary inability to prevent them from doing so. Because if you are willing to fight a war, none of them, great or small, can resist you." **5.** In the peroration, another reference to war achievements is useful: "I do not want any of you to forget the recent triumphs for which you are already famous today. Because, in every respect, in the power of the body, but also in the power of the soul, and in the manufacture of weapons, we stand out from them."

50.1. It is also advisable, after the peroration, to ask the opinion of the army[85] and, if they agree with the idea of war, to praise them for their intentions; but if they do not do so immediately, then the general should by all means avoid the possibility of rejecting the war, and push them to face the conflict with courage. For example, he may ask: "And now what should we do? Will we support the war or will we avoid the battle?" And if the soldiers are prone to idleness, it is good to add the following: "In no way could this happen, that is, to avoid battle. It is worse then trying to keep the enemies away. Better let us

---

83 *ἐπίλογος*: reasoning, inference; peroration of a speech.

84 *ἀλλοφύλων*, from *ἀλλόφυλος*: of another tribe, foreign.

85 According to the author of the text, the general can ask for the opinion of his soldiers, thus making them participants, albeit perhaps ostensibly, in the decision-making process. This could boost morale, especially when the general conditions are favourable, although we do not know of any specific incident where this practice was applied, and if so what the reaction of the troops was or its effect on their combat performance. This practice is repeated as advice in the *Naumachica* (Syrianos' Naval Battles, paragraphs 18–19. In *Naumachica of Leo VI, Maurice, Syrianos Magister, Basil Patrikios, Nikephoros Ouranos* [Athens: Kanake, 2005]).

rise to the challenge and hurry to attack them." **2.** Furthermore, it is necessary to express this last call for war with not a long speech. **3.** In fact, the encouragement should be fervently enthusiastic, uttered in short sentences, full of hope, so that the words and the figures of speech would awaken the listeners, for example: "Let us stand up, take up arms, throw ourselves at the enemies, smash our opponents, make up for their initial advantage, so that full of joy we can make a happy return, wearing crowns of glory, holding in our hands the rewards of our labours, which we will obtain with the help of God. This is how things are for me: we trust in Him, we are guided by Him, and with His help we will overcome our enemies."

51. It is, therefore, necessary for the general, during his speech, to use other means of expression, but stay away from ruggedness[86] and vehemence,[87] unless the speaker is one who enjoys the admiration of his listeners because of his martial skills, but also because his advice and what he did was always in favour of the salvation of the audience, as Odysseus calls the Achaeans "Achaeadas," an adjective that has a vehemence, which he used not because he was disgusted, but because he wanted to rouse[88] them to battle.

52.1. Public speeches that have a rough and vehement style are served in one way, when not all those present are reprimanded, but also those to whom the rebuke is directed are not named, for example: "That is why, O children and brothers, I feel so positive towards you that I do not want to hear about deeds that were done and were contrary to the will of God, or on the other hand, were not useful to those who did them. **2.** But, since I have heard many others say that among you are some who are indifferent to the battle with the enemy or are not interested in the salvation of their compatriots, things that if God will not prevent, then the danger will become unbearable for us, I convened this meeting, to speak to you and to urge you to do what the laws require, to which we should all obey, even if we do not want to. **3.** And let none of you say: 'I personally know nothing about all this.' It is clear that most of you are strangers to such things. **4.** It is absolutely necessary to approach those who are involved in such thoughts and actions, omitting their names, and before we punish them let us try to bring them back to reason, not blaming you who are the most rational, for failing to persuade them to come to their senses before we even speak to them." **5.** Secondly, it is useful to speak, not openly, but as if we have heard these things through others, for example "So I do not want you, my dear soldiers, to ignore what others are saying against you. **6.** It is said that every craftsman cares for the things that belong to

---

86 τραχύτης: roughness, ruggedness.
87 σφοδρότης: vehemence, violence.
88 διεγείρων, from ἐγείρω: awaken, rouse.

him, for example the farmer cares for the plough and the yoke, the mare and the oxen and the work in the field, the gardener in the same way for the digger, the good condition of plants and the pruning of trees, sailors care for the sail, the oar, the anchor and the rudder, and even women care for the spindle, the rocket and the wool, but the soldier cares not for his own things, neither his weapons, his horses, his exercises nor anything else that gives him more prestige and helps him achieve a glorious result in war. **7.** But what do they do instead? They stay at home and sleep, gamble, tell tall tales, brag, while when they are on campaign they do not try to find the enemy, nor do they rush against him, nor do they motivate others to do so, but they look around in secret how to find a way to escape from the enemies and hide. **8.** I do not think nor have I ever said such things about you. How can any of you have such thoughts, let alone the will to put them to action, when this would bring the enemy closer not only to us, but also to our women and our children and our fields, reasons why our enemies are attacking, precisely because we do not want to react? **9.** The farther we try to get away from the enemies, the more courage they take and pursue us all the way to our own doorstep."

53.1. The prelude to such speeches should have such a content that they do not upset the listeners too much, for example: "Many detest the exhortations and hate reproaches,[89] not knowing that there is nothing else that conquers over pain and is useful in life, for this is precisely what parents do for their children. They urge them, scold them, sometimes flog them, not because they hate them, not as enemies, but because they care for them. **2.** So, like the father is to his children, so is the general to his troops: he rejoices in their achievements, but he mourns and weeps for their ruin. In fact, whatever he does, he does it for them, so that if they make mistakes, they can correct themselves, and if they live the right way and become better, then they become better men and are more worthy of glory than others are."

54.1. It is not only the exhortative speech that excites soldiers and makes them more eager for war, but other speeches as well, such as the triumphal,[90] the consolatory[91] and the reproach.[92] **2.** The triumphal speech is uttered when, after a victory against the enemies, we celebrate with brilliance the happy outcome of the confrontation, the consolatory when, although we fought with all our might, we are ultimately defeated by the enemies, while the reproach when our troops are defeated, having demonstrated slackness or disorder, or having made other similar mistakes.

---

89 ἔλεγχος: reproach, disgrace, dishonour.
90 ἐπινίκιος: of victory.
91 παραμυθητικός: consolatory.
92 τραχύς: rough, harsh, savage, to be rough, harshly disposed.

55.1. When delivering a triumphal speech, we must begin by thanking God, to whom the present victory is due, then thank the emperor for doing what he ought to strengthen us, and thirdly the soldiers for their discipline and their efforts on the field of battle. **2.** Praise God in this manner: "Men, brothers, fellow-soldiers, it is proper before anything else to thank God, through Whom we have acquired so many other goods, but above all the victory over our enemies, and the crowns with which we celebrate the achievement of this triumph." **3.** We then thank the ruler in this way: "It is fair to thank our emperor for many different reasons, but also because of his solicitude for us." **4.** To the soldiers, then, if the general is giving a speech to them: "I am also grateful for your virtues, the zeal you showed, the passion, the bravery, the perseverance, the fact that you fought as befits heroes and, seeing this, God rewarded you with victory." **5.** It is appropriate, after all these thanks, first to praise them all together, and then those who displayed excellence on the battlefield by name, then once again return to the common praise for the whole army, and finally make the present victory look like the foundation stone for future military successes.

56.1. In the consolatory speech, when we have to comfort the defeated soldiers, we emphasize from the beginning that the defeat did not occur out of cowardice, but because of the numerical superiority of the enemy, or by a game of chance, or for reasons of topography, for example: "Perhaps, soldiers, the enemies think that it was through our cowardice, or through their own display of bravery, that they were victorious today. But I know, and I am fully convinced, that this happened neither out of our own cowardice nor out of their own bravery, but due to the fact that they were superior in numbers, or because the ground they chose was more favourable to them." **2.** Then, thirdly, we must tell the soldiers that even if God punished them for something bad they did in their lives, if they choose to be in God's way again, then He too will fight with them for redress. **3.** And the emperor can resort to another innovation, that is, to transfer the responsibilities of defeat from the soldiers to the general. **4.** Finally, it is necessary to say that, although we suffered what we suffered, from now on this will be useful in the course of the war, as the enemy will underestimate us and thus may conduct military operations more carelessly, and this will make us safer, giving us the opportunity to fight harder against them. **5.** This position can also be constructed in this way, especially when we can resort to an example from history itself, when those who won first and then underestimated the enemies were defeated in a second battle, while, on the other hand, those who initially were defeated, then showed caution, became stronger and won the second clash. **6.** For example, Arvakes the Mede and Cyrus the Persian ultimately proved victorious, the first against the Assyrians and the second against the Medes.

57.1. The reproach speech is to some extent inspired by the consolatory, which is why it is closely related to it, as both of them urge a future display of courage. **2.** For you must not only rebuke those who have been defeated because of sluggishness in battle, but at the same time comfort them, and through consolation and exhortation motivate them to war, saying for example: "I do not know how you soldiers feel, for what reasons you fought so badly, or have not fought at all (indeed, one might have said, looking at you, that you betrayed victory to the enemy), but I ache in soul and body when I think how we will return so dishonourably to our homes, and face our people, our wives and children, our friends and our neighbours, and what those who envy you will have to say. **3.** I know very well that they will turn to each other and make fun of us by saying: 'Where are the words and the promises and the boasting of our soldiers? Where are the general's testimonies and praises for the soldiers? Were are they empty hopes that were placed on them?' **4.** These are words that hurt my heart and discourage me, like a sword that tears my body, hearing such words I would rather die than live. **5.** Indeed, if you were unable to stand up to the enemies, we have certainly suffered, but not so much as to seek death. **6.** And now, why do we suffer? We suffer because, while you could have defeated the enemy, you chose to show them your backs, and the dense tears drip down my chest, splash, and wash away the affection I have for you. **7.** See how much frustration you have caused us, what words you have caused us to say? What situation could be more difficult than this? What is more sorrowful than such speeches that make you and me sad? **8.** So is there any solace and cure for these words, that can make this heart disease, if I can call it that, go away? **9.** It is clear that it exists, but not if we flee like birds away from the enemy or run away like deer to the mountains to escape danger. After all, what is so terrible to see or impossible for men fighting with weapons against other men, when many times we have seen women do things that are appropriate for men, even though the opposite has happened now?"

Example of a consolatory speech, in the absence of the transposition[93] of the cause [when the reproach takes place, then the transposition of the cause is missing]

58. "So it is possible, O men, if we wish, to get rid of this frustration through our struggle, and to bring humiliation to the opponents. Because, indeed, frequently many who won many victories ended up being defeated, and on the contrary, many who repeatedly lost finally managed to prevail over their previous victors."

---

93 μετάθεσις: change of position, transposition.

Bibliography

A Primary sources

Chatzelis, Georgios and Jonathan Harris (trans.), *A Tenth-Century Byzantine Military Manual: The Sylloge Tacticorum* (Oxon and New York: Routledge, 2017)

Constantine Porphyrogennitos, *De Administrando Imperio* (Greek text), G. Moravcsik (ed.) and R. J. H. Jenkins (trans.) (Washington, DC: Dumbarton Oaks, 1985)

Constantine Porphyrogennitos, *Three Treatises on Imperial Military Expeditions*, John F. Haldon (ed. and trans.) (Vienna: Verlag der Österreichischen Akademie der Wissenschaften, 1990)

Corazzini, F., *Scritto sulla Tattica Navale di Anonimo Greco* (Livorno: Vannini, 1883)

Dain, A., *Naumachica* (Paris: Les Belles Lettres, 1943)

Demetroukas, I. Ch., *Ναυμαχικά Λέοντος Στ´, Μαυρικίου, Συριανού Μαγίστρου, Βασιλείου Πατρικίου, Νικηφόρου Ουρανού* [*Naumachica of Leo VI, Maurice, Syrianos Magister, Basil Patrikios, Nikephoros Ouranos*] (Athens: Kanake, 2005)

Dennis, George T. (trans.), *Maurice's Strategikon, Handbook of Byzantine Military Strategy* (Philadelphia: University of Pennsylvania Press, 1984)

Dennis, George T., *Three Byzantine Military Treatises*, CFHB: 25 (Washington, DC: Dumbarton Oaks, 1985/2008 (repr.))

Dennis, George T. (ed. and trans.), *The Taktika of Leo VI* (Washington, DC: Dumbarton Oaks, 2010)

Kekaumenos, *Strategikon*, Dimitrios Tsougkarakes (trans.) (Athens: Agrostis, Kanake, 1993)

Mango, Cyril and Roger Scott (trans.), *The Chronicle of Theophanes Confessor* (Oxford: Clarendon, 1997)

Sullivan, Denis (ed. and trans.), *The Rise and Fall of Nikephoros II Phokas, Five Contemporary Texts in Annotated Translations* (Leiden: Brill, 2019)

B Secondary sources

Ahrweiler, H., "Un discours inédit de Constantin VII Porphyrogénète," *Travaux et Mémoires* 2 (1967), 393–404

Anson, Edward, "The General's Pre-Battle Exhortation in Graeco-Roman Warfare," *Greece & Rome* 57 (2010), 304–18

Bliese, John R. E., "Fighting Spirit and Literary Genre: A Comparison of Battle Exhortations in the 'Song of Roland' and in Chronicles of the Central Middle Ages," *Neuphilologische Mitteilungen* 96 (1995), 417–36

Christides, Vasilios, "The Raids of the Moslems of Crete in the Aegean Sea, Piracy and Conquest," *Byzantion* 51 (1981), 76–111

Cosentino, S., "The Syrianos' Strategikon – A 9th-Century Source?" *Bizantinistica: Rivista di Studi Bizantini e Slavi* 2 (2000), 243–80

Dain, Alphonse, *La "Tactique" de Nicéphore Ouranos* (Paris: Les Belles Lettres, 1937)

Dain, Alphonse, "Les Stratégistes Byzantins," *Travaux et Mémoires* 2 (1967), 317–92

Dain, Alphonse, "Luc Holste et la 'Collection Romaine' des Tacticiens grecs," *Revue des Études Anciennes* 71 (1969), 338–53

Eramo, Imma, "ᵀΩ ἄνδρες στρατιῶται: Demegorie protrettiche nell'Ambrosianus B 119 sup.," *Annali della Facoltà di Lettere e Filosofia dell'Università degli Studi di Bari* 50 (2007), 127–65

Eramo, Imma, "Retorica militare fra tradizione protrettica e pensiero strategico," *Talia Dixit: Revista Interdisciplinar de Retórica e Historiografía* 5 (2010), 25–44

Eramo, Imma, *Siriano Discorsi di Guerra* (Bari: Dedalo, 2010)

Eramo, Imma, "On Syrianus Magister's Military Compendium," *Classica et Christiana* 7 (2012), 97–116

Frendo, Joseph D. C., "History and Panegyric in the Age of Heraclius: The Literary Background to the Composition of the 'Histories' of Theophylact Simocatta," *Dumbarton Oaks Papers* 42 (1988), 143–56

Haldon, John F., *A Critical Commentary on the Taktika of Leo VI* (Washington, DC: Dumbarton Oaks, 2014)

Hammond, N. G. L., *Three Historians of Alexander the Great: The So-Called Vulgate Authors, Diodorus, Justin and Curtius* (Cambridge: Cambridge University Press, 1983)

Hansen, Mogens Herman, "The Battle Exhortation in Ancient Historiography: Fact or Fiction?," *Historia: Zeitschrift für Alte Geschichte* 42 (1993), 161–80

Hansen, Mogens Herman, "The Little Grey Horse: Henry V's Speech at Agincourt and the Battle Exhortation in Ancient Historiography," *Histos* 2 (1998), 46–63

Iglesias Zoido, Juan Carlos, "The Battle Exhortation in Ancient Rhetoric," *Rhetorica* 25 (2007), 141–58

Iglesias Zoido, Juan Carlos, "The Pre-Battle Speeches of Alexander at Issus and Gaugamela," *Greek, Roman, and Byzantine Studies* 50 (2010), 215–41

Kaldellis, Anthony, *Procopius of Caesarea: Tyranny, History, and Philosophy at the End of Antiquity* (Philadelphia, PA: University of Pennsylvania Press, 2004)

Karaple, Konstantina, "Speeches of Arab Leaders to Their Warriors According to Byzantine Texts," *Graeco-Arabica* 5 (1993), 233–42

Karaple, Konstantina, *Κατευόδωσις στρατού: Η οργάνωση και η ψυχολογική προετοιμασία του βυζαντινού στρατού πριν από τον πόλεμο (610–1081) [Kateuodosis*

Stratou: The Organization and Mental Preparation of the Byzantine Army Before War (610–1081)] (Athens: Myrmidones, 2010)

Kolia-Dermitzaki, Athena, "Η ιδέα του 'ιερού πολέμου' στο Βυζάντιο κατά τον 10ο αιώνα. Η μαρτυρία των τακτικών και των δημηγοριών" [The Idea of 'Holy War' in Byzantium in the 10th Century: The Testimony of the Taktika and the Harangues], in: *Κωνσταντίνος Ζ΄ ο Πορφυρογέννητος και η εποχή του, Β΄ Διεθνής Βυζαντινολογική Συνάντηση, Δελφοί, 22–26 Ιουλίου 1987* (Athens: NHRF, 1989), 39–55

Kolia-Dermitzaki, Athena, "Το Εμπόλεμο Βυζάντιο στις Ομιλίες και τις Επιστολές του 10ου και 11ου αι. – μια Ιδεολογική Προσέγγιση" [Byzantium at War in the Speeches and Letter of the 10th and 11th Centuries – an Ideological Approach], in: K. Tsiknakes (ed.), *Byzantium at War (9th–12th Centuries)* (Athens: NHRF, 1997), 213–38

Kolias, Taxiarches G., "Η πολεμική τακτική των βυζαντινών: θεωρία και πράξη" [The Military Tactics of the Byzantines: Theory and Practice], in: N. Oikonomides (ed.), *Byzantium at War (9th–12th Century)* (Athens: National Research Foundation, 1997), 153–64

Kotlowska, Anna and Łukasz Rozycki, "The Role and Place of Speeches in the Work of Theophylact Simocatta," *Vox Patrum* 36 (2016), 353–82

Lee, A. D. and J. Shepard, "A Double Life: Placing the Peri Presbeon," *Byzantino-Slavica* 52 (1991), 15–39

Lendon, Jon E., "Battle Description in the Ancient Historians, Part II: Speeches, Results, and Sea Battles," *Greece and Rome* 64 (2017), 145–67

Lounghis, Tilemachos, *Byzantium in Eastern Mediterranean: Safeguarding East Roman Identity (407–1204)* (Nicosia: Cyprus Research Centre, 2010)

Lounghis, Tilemachos, "The Byzantine War Navy and the West, Fifth to Twelfth Centuries," in: Georgios Theotokis and Aysel Yildiz (eds.), *A Military History of the Mediterranean Sea: Aspects of War, Diplomacy and Military Elites* (Leiden: Brill, 2018), 21–43

Markopoulos, Anastasios, "The Ideology of War in the Military Harangues of Constantine VII Porphyrogennetos," in: J. Koder and I. Stouraitis (eds.), *Byzantine War Ideology Between Roman Imperial Concept and Christian Religion, Akten des Internationalen Symposiums (Wien, 19–21 Mai 2011)* (Vienna: Austrian Academy of Sciences Press, 2012), 47–56

Mazzucchi, Carlo M., "Dagli anni di Basilio Parakimomenos (cod. Ambr. B 119 sup.)," *Aevum* 52 (1978), 267–316

McCormick, Matthew, *Eternal Victory, Triumphal Rulership in Late Antiquity, Byzantium, and the Early Medieval West* (Cambridge: Cambridge University Press, 1986)

McGeer, Eric, *Sowing the Dragon's Teeth: Byzantine Warfare in the Tenth Century* (Washington, DC: Dumbarton Oaks, 1995)

McGeer, Eric, "Two Military Orations of Constantine VII," in: J. W. Nesbitt (ed.), *Byzantine Authors: Literary Activities and Preoccupations. Texts and Translations Dedicated to the Memory of Nicolas Oikonomides* (Leiden and Boston: Brill, 2003), 111–38

Mpezentakos, Nikolaos, *Η Ρητορική της Ομηρικής Μάχης* [*The Rhetoric of Homeric Battle*] (Athens: Kardamitsa, 1996)

Müller, K. K., *Eine griechische Schrift über Seekrieg* (Würzburg, 1882)

Nordling, John G., "Caesar's Pre-Battle Speech at Pharsalus (B.C. 3.85.4): *Ridiculum Acri Fortius . . . Secat Res*," *The Classical Journal* 101 (2005/2006), 183–9

Pritchett, W. K., "The General's Exhortations," in: *Essays in Greek History* (Amsterdam: J.C. Gieben, 1994), 27–109

Pryor, J. H. and E. M. Jeffreys, *The Age of the ΔΡΟΜΩΝ: The Byzantine Navy ca. 500–1204* (Leiden: Brill, 2006)

Rance, Philip, "The Date of the Military Compendium of Syrianus Magister (Formerly the Sixth-Century *Anonymus Byzantinus*)," *Byzantinische Zeitschrift* 100 (2007), 701–37

Rance, Philip, "The Reception of Aineias' Poliorketika in Byzantine Military Literature," in: Maria Pretzler and Nick Barley (eds.), *Brill's Companion to Aineias Tacticus* (Leiden: Brill, 2017), 290–374

Riedel, Meredith L. D., "Biblical Echoes in Two Byzantine Military Speeches," *Byzantine and Modern Greek Studies* 40 (2016), 207–22

Riedel, Meredith L. D., *Leo VI and the Transformation of Byzantine Christian Identity: Writings of an Unexpected Emperor* (Cambridge: Cambridge University Press, 2018)

Slaughter, Francess, "Direct and Indirect Speeches in Tacitus' *Historiae*" (Unpublished MA thesis, University of Richmond, Richmond, 1974)

Stouraitis, Yannis, *Krieg und Frieden in der politischen und ideologischen Wahrnehmung in Byzanz (7–11 Jahrhundert)*. Byzantinische Geschichtsschreiber, 5 (Vienna: Fassbaender, 2009)

Stouraitis, Yannis, " 'Just War' and 'Holy War' in the Middle Ages: Rethinking Theory Through the Byzantine Case-Study," *Jahrbuch der Österreichischen Byzantinistik* 62 (2013), 227–64

Stouraitis, Yannis, "State War Ethic and Popular Views on Warfare," in: Yannis Stouraitis (ed.), *A Companion to the Byzantine Culture of War, ca. 300–1204* (Leiden: Brill, 2018), 59–91

Stouraitis, Yannis, "Using the Bible to Justify Imperial Warfare in High-Medieval Byzantium," in: C. Rapp and A. Kulzer (eds.), *The Bible in Byzantium: Appropriation, Adaptation, Interpretation: Journal of Ancient Judaism Supplements*, vol. 25, no. 6 (Vienna: Vandenhoeck & Ruprecht, 2018), 89–106

Taragna, A. M., "Λόγος Πόλεμος: eloquenza e persuasione nei trattati bizantini di arte militare," in: T. Creazzo and G. Strano (eds.), *Atti del VI Congresso nazionale dell: Associazione Italiana di Studi Bizantini, Catania-Messina, 2–5 ottobre 2000. Numero speciale di Siculorum Gymnasium n. s.*, vol. 57 (Catania, 2004), 797–810

Theotokis, Georgios, *Byzantine Military Tactics in Syria and Mesopotamia in the Tenth Century, a Comparative Study* (Edinburgh: Edinburgh University Press, 2018)

Whately, Conor, *Battles and Generals: Combat, Culture, and Didacticism in Procopius' Wars* (Leiden: Brill, 2016)

Wiita, J. E., "The Ethnika in Byzantine Military Treatises" (Unpublished PhD diss., University of Minnesota, Minneapolis 1977)

Yellin, Keith, *Battle Exhortation: The Rhetoric of Combat Leadership* (Columbia, SC: University of South Carolina Press, 2008)

Zuckerman, C., "The Military Compendium of Syrianus Magister," *Jahrbuch der Österreichischen Byzantinistik* 40 (1990), 209–24

Index - introduction

Abbasid(s) 11, 12n50; Egypt 16;
    governor of Tarsus 13
Abu'l Asair, Sayf ad-Dawla's cousin
    7n25
adlocūtiō 31
Aegean Sea 14–16, 18; *theme* 16
Aelian 4, 9, 21, 22n84
Aeneas Tacticus 11, 22, 25;
    Poliorketika 11
Ambrosianus B-119-sup 3, 9, 10, 27, 28
Amorion 12; 42 Martyrs of 12; siege
    and sack of 11, 12, 12n49, 12n50, 13
Anzen, Battle of 11, 12
Apollodoros of Damascus 22
Arabs (Ἄραβες) 7n26, 8, 13, 14, 42, 53;
    "African" 18; Cretan 16–18, 27, 39;
    Sicilian 19–20
Argyros, Eustathios 20
Asclepiodotos 9, 22n84, 25

Barberinianus graecus 59, 27
Basil I 5, 7, 14, 15, 17, 19, 21
Basil the *parakoimomenos* 27
Belisarius 6–8, 35, 74n67
Bernensis 97 27

Caesar 30, 39
calcatio 7n25
Capture of Crete by Theodosios the
    Deacon 40
Constantine VII 4, 20, 26, 42; *De*
    Administrando Imperio 20, 42; *De*
    Ceremoniis Aulae Byzantinae 7;
    Imperial exhortations 40–2, 44, 52;
    Imperial Military Expeditions 47

Cosentino, Salvatore 3, 6, 8–10, 21
Crete 14, 15, 16, 18, 20, 21, 27, 39
Cyprus 14, 15, 16, 20, 21

Dain, Alphonse 2, 3, 26
Damietta 17
droungarios (land army) 36n155
droungarios of the fleet 14, 18, 19, 20,
    21

Ephemios 18

George of Pisidia 32, 32n135
Ghassanid 8

Hellas, theme of 17
heralds (= καντατόρων) 37
Hermogenes of Tarsus 22, 23, 24, 25
Herodotus 29
Holste, Lukas 2, 2n5, 27
Homer 29, 37

Idistavisto Battle of 30
Justinian 6, 66n43
Justinian II 15

Kekaumenos 23, 38, 47, 51;
    Strategikon 47, 51
Kibyrrhaeotae, theme of 15, 16, 16n65,
    19, 20
Köchly, Hermann 2, 6, 7, 8, 26, 27, 28

Lalakaon River, Battle of 13
Lascaris Janus 26
Lascaris-Leontaris Demetrios 26

Leo III 5
Leo the Deacon 39, 41
List of Precedence (Klētorologion) of
    Philotheos 5
Louis II, Holy Roman Emperor 19
Lounghis, Tilemachos 14, 15, 16, 18,
    19, 20
lustratio exercitus 31, 31n138

Marcellinus, Ammianus 31, 39
Marcianus graecus 976.1 28
Mardaites 20
Mediceo-Laurentianus graecus, 55.4 25
Medici Lorenzo de 26
Melitene 13, 15
Michael II 11, 12, 16
Michael III 5, 11, 12, 13, 13n54, 16, 18
Military Precepts by Nikephoros
    Phokas 54
Mons Graupius, Battle of 30
Musele, Alexios 18

Naser (Nasr) 19
Naumachiae by Syrianos 1, 2, 3, 4, 10,
    11, 14, 28, 36
North Africa 6, 42

Oiniates 17
Onasander 4, 25; *Στρατηγικός/General*
    38, 38n163, 51
On Skirmishing 38, 41, 44, 52
On Strategy (De re strategica) 1–9,
    21–4, 27–8, 37, 46
Ooryphas Niketas 18, 19

Parisinus graecus 2446 27
Parisinus graecus 2522 26, 55
Paulicians of Tephrike 7, 13, 15
phalanx 3, 22, 23
Phokas, Nikephoros the Elder 20

Poliorketika by Philo of Byzantium 22
Polyaenus 4, 39, 39n172
Polybius 28, 30; *Histories* 28n120
Poseidonius of Apameia 9
Procopius 35, 74n67
Progymnasmata by Aphthonius 22–4
prōtomagistros 5

Rance, Philip 2, 6, 8, 9, 10, 11, 22, 25,
    26, 27
Romanos II 39
Rüstow, Wilhelm 2, 6, 7

Sicily 14, 15, 18, 19, 20, 21
Simokattes, Theophylaktos 32
Stouraitis 9, 12, 32, 45, 46, 48, 49, 52
Strategemata by Sextus Julius
    Frontinus 38
Strategikon by Maurice 10, 38, 43, 48,
    51, 54
suasōria 30
Sylloge Taktikorum 38n167, 51, 54

Tactical Constitutions by Leo VI 4, 6,
    10, 14, 15, 20, 21, 36, 39, 43, 50, 52;
    'Constitution 19' 10, 14, 21
Tactical Theory by Aelian 21, 22
Taktikon Uspensky 19
Theoktistos 16
Theophilos 11, 12, 13, 18, 21
Thucydides 29–30
tribunal 32
Tyrteus 29

Vindobonensis phil. graecus 275 4

Xenophon 30n130, 37n162

Zuckerman, Constantine 22, 22n84,
    23–4, 24nn93–4

Index - translation

Aelius Aristides 62n26
Agathias 66n43
argument 69, 72, 74, 76, 83
Aristides 60
Arvakes (the Mede) 86
Athenians 63, 72, 80, 81

case (προβολή) 59,
    60n17
Christ 62, 75
Cyrus (the Persian) 86

development 60, 82
Dionysios 72

Goths 66n43
Greeks 66n43

Lazika 66n43

Martinus 66n43
Medes 86

Olynthians 63

Peisistratos 72
Phasis, city of 66n43
phalanx 78, 79
Phokion/Fokion 67, 67n47
position (κεφάλαιον) 60, 69, 82, 86,
    87n93
preamble (προκατάστασις) 59, 60, 70, 82
preface (προκατασκευή) 59, 60
preliminary exposition (προδιήγησις)
    59, 82
prelude (προοίμιον) 59, 82, 85
proposition 60, 82

question 55, 58, 58n11, 60, 82

Romans 66, 72, 73, 74n67, 76, 77

syllogism 60, 69, 74, 82

Telon (the Athenian) 82

Vandals 66n43

Zopyros (the Persian) 82

Index - Greek terms

δημηγορία 1, 29
δημηγορίαι προτρεπτικαί 35
ἐπιπώλησις 29

παραίνεσις 29
παράκλησις 29
σκουταρῶμα (Latin "scutum") 9